KETO DIET COOKBOOK FOR WOMEN AFTER 50:

200 Delicious & Easy to Prepare Recipes Perfect for Fat Loss +60 Days Meal Plan.

© Copyright 2020 - All rights reserved.

Disclaimer Notice:

Please note the information contained within this document is for educational and entertainment purposes only. All effort has been executed to present accurate, up to date, and reliable, complete information. No warranties of any kind are declared or implied. Readers acknowledge that the author is not engaging in the rendering of legal, financial, medical or professional advice. The content within this book has been derived from various sources. Please consult a licensed professional before attempting any techniques outlined in this book.

By reading this document, the reader agrees that under no circumstances is the author responsible for any losses, direct or indirect, which are incurred as a result of the use of information contained within this document, including, but not limited to, errors, omissions, or inaccuracies.

TABLE OF CONTENTS

Introduction

As women, when our age grows at 50, we are always looking for a quick and effective way to shed our excess weight, get our high blood sugar levels under control, reduce overall inflammation, and improve our physical and mental energy. It's frustrating to have all of these issues, especially the undeniable fats in our belly. Good thing that I found this great solution to all our worries when we reach this age level, and when our body gets weaker as time goes by. The Ketogenic diet plans.

As a woman at this age, we all know that it is much more difficult for us to lose weight than men. I have lived on a starvation level diet and exercise like a triathlete and only lose five pounds. A man will stop putting dressing on his salad and will lose twenty pounds. It just not fair. But we have the fact that we are women to blame. Women naturally have more standing between ourselves and weight loss than men do.

The mere fact that we, women, is the largest single contributor to why we find it difficult to lose weight. Since our bodies always think it needs to be prepared for a possible pregnancy, we will naturally have more body fat and less mass in our muscles than men.

Being in menopause will also cause us to add more pounds to our bodies, especially in the lower half. After menopause, our metabolism naturally slows down. Our hormones levels will decrease. These two factors alone will cause weight gain in the post-menopausal period.

There are numerous diet plan options offered to help shed weight, but the Ketogenic diet has been the most preferred lately. We've got many concerns around keto's effectiveness and exactly how to follow the diet plan in a healthy and balanced means.

The ketogenic diet for ladies at the age or over 50 is an easy and ideal way to shed extra pounds, stay energetic, and enjoy a healthy life. It does not only balances hormones but also improves our body capabilities without causing any harm to our overall wellness. Thus, if you are fighting with post-menopausal symptoms and other health issues, you should do a Keto diet right away!

A Keto diet is a lifestyle, not a diet so, treat it like the same. The best way to approach keto to gain maximum benefits, especially for women over 50s, is to treat it as a lifestyle. You can't restrict your meal intake through obstructive and strict diets forever, right? It's the fundamental reason fad diets fail — we limit ourselves from too much to get rapid results, then we're are right back again at the weight where we started, or God forbid worse.

Keto is not a kind of diet that can be followed strictly forever — unless you need it as a therapeutic diet (i.e., epilepsy), a very narrow category. In keto diet, we slowly transit into a curative state that we can withstand forever in a healthier way.

So, for me, being on a keto diet does not mean that I will be in ketosis forever. Instead, it means letting myself love consideration, such as a few desserts while vacationing or partying. It does not set me back to enjoy these desserts and let me consider it as the end of the diet. I can wake up the following morning and go back to the keto lifestyle, most suitable for me and my body consistently.

It allows my body to boost its fat loss drastically in many cases, which helps in decreasing pockets of undesirable fat.

With Keto Diet, it's not only giving weight loss assistance to reduce my weight, yet it can likewise ward off yearnings for unhealthy foods and protect me against calories collisions throughout the day. That is why I want it to share with you how promising this Keto diet. As our age grow older, we must not let our body do the same. Focus your mindset on this fantastic diet, read, apply, and enjoy its best benefits.

What I promise you after you read the full guide of Keto Diet for Women after 50 and apply it to your daily lifestyle, especially the 30 days meal plan, you will achieve more than losing weight but also the new and improve healthier you.

CHAPTER 1:

What is the Keto Diet?

The ketogenic diet is straightforward in its execution, objective: remain in Ketosis; in any case, the way can be distinctive for every individual. Everybody starts at 20 pure sugars and afterward, after some time, decides what the number of they can expand without being kicked out of Ketosis. I've taken more than 75 net carbs in a day and remained in Ketosis while my significant other, who adhered to his diet and had two chomps, was kicked out of Ketosis. Everybody is different. It's up to each person of us to realize what our own "Kick Out" point is and remain beneath it. To figure pure sugars, take the number of starches you devour and subtract the number of fiber grams expended. It is the number you'll use to follow your day by day complete. At the point when nourishment is high in fiber, similar to coconut, you can eat a more significant amount of it regardless of whether the sugar numbers look somewhat terrifying. When alluding to macros, I'm talking about the equalization of nourishments you eat in a day. They can be categorized as one of the three fundamental macronutrient classes: sugars, proteins, and fat. A few people on the keto diet find that these rates are useful for monitoring their weight reduction and others use them for therapeutic reasons.

There are many number crunchers online that you can use to enter your details, such as weight, stature, sex, weight objective, etc. The adding machine will mention what should be the perfect full scale for you. The measure of carbs (which should, by and large, originate from vegetables) or fats will make Ketosis in the body shifts for various individuals. It is unquestionably not an exact science.

For this guide's plans, the large-scale rates were determined by taking the number of grams of every full scale and duplicating it by the number of calories per gram (9 calories for 1 gram of fat, four calories for 1 gram of carbs or proteins). Afterward, partitioning that by the all outnumber of calories per serving. For instance, envision a dish that has the accompanying nutritional data per serving:

Calories: 184; Total Fat: 14g; Saturated Fat: 6g; Cholesterol: 224mg;

Sugars: 2g; Fiber: 1g; Net Carbs: 1g; Protein: 12g

To decide the number of a serving's calories, originate from fat:

(14 grams of fat) × (9 calories for every gram of fat) = 126 calories from fat

(126 calories from fat for every serving) ÷ (184 complete calories for every serving) = 68.5%

To decide the number of a serving's calories, originate from protein:

(12 grams of protein) × (4 calories for every gram of protein) = 48 calories from protein

(48 calories from protein for every serving) ÷ (184 all-out calories for each meal) = 26%

Each meal you eat doesn't have to follow these macros; you make a count by the day's end. It enables you to eat a dish of vegetables sautéed in ghee without the need to toss in pancetta.

As you counsel, the macros for every formula in this guide, know that there's a variety among various fixings. For instance, substantial natural cream may have less than one net carb, while a non-natural store-brand may have more. Tomato sauce is another dubious one. Some better assortments of marinara come in as low as four net carbs per ¼ cup since they contain no additional sugar, yet most standard brands have at least 15 net carbs in that equivalent ¼ cup. To appreciate an Italian fix every so often, I suggest spending too much on the great stuff or making your very own sauce.

Even though the ketogenic diet isn't intended to be exclusionary, and you could surely get your 20 net carbs every day from a solitary cut of bread. You presumably won't make it far in a ketogenic way of life. Your glucose will spike and probably show you out of Ketosis, and it won't be any good times. Attempt instead of some rich veggies and obey-gooey fondue, and that cut of bread won't be vital. Keep a watch out: Before long, you will lose your desires for bread!

Benefits of Keto Diet for Women after 50

Loss and Maintenance of Weight

Gaining extra pounds (especially around the abdomen) and struggling with controlling the weight are common nuisances that menopausal and post-menopausal women have to deal with. As you can already imagine, this age-related problem is also a result of the decline in estrogen levels.

Going Keto can help you lose weight and burn fat in a couple of ways

Going Keto Decreases Your Appetite

Going Keto Leads to Rapid Weight Loss

Control of Glucose in the Body

Science has found out that decreased estrogen levels can promote insulin resistance, and in turn, increase the blood sugar. Having an insulin resistance, your body is practically immune to the effects of insulin.

A reduction in Reliance on the Medications-related to Diabetes

With Keto, you drastically limit your carbs and sugars consumption. With little blood sugar, your body does not need to release insulin to manage it. Thus, you prevent developing diabetes symptoms. If you already have it, the diet helps you to order it.

Control of High Blood Pressure

Once you attain 50, you must monitor your blood pressure rates. Reduction in the intake of carbohydrates is a proven way to lower your blood pressure. When you cut down on your carbs and lower your blood sugar levels, you significantly reduce your chances of getting other diseases.

An Improved mental performance

The keto diet provides your body and brain with a stable fuel source – ketones. The diet prevents sugar swings that are associated with a carb-rich diet. That allows you to avoid brain fog, improves your focus, concentration, and mental clarity.

Restoration of Insulin Sensitivity

That is the first objective of a keto diet. It helps stabilize the insulin levels and thereby improve fat burning. Using a keto diet helps preserve your muscles while burning fat in your body.

Improve Cholesterol Levels

It will help reduce blood cholesterol levels by consuming fewer carbohydrates while on the keto diet. That is due to the increased lipolysis condition. That leads to lower levels of LDL cholesterol and higher levels of HDL cholesterol.

Satiety

Eating protein reduces the ghrelin (the hunger hormone) and stimulates the production of the satiety hormones. When you eat protein, it's transformed into amino acids, which help your body with various processes such as building muscle and regulating immune function

CHAPTER 2:

Best Keto-Friendly Foods

Cheese

The cheese is delicious and nutritious. Thankfully, although there are many sorts of cheese out there, they are low in carbs and filled with fat. Eating cheese may even help your muscles and hamper aging.

Avocados

Avocados are so famous nowadays within the health community that folks associate the word "health" to avocados. This way is often for an excellent reason because avocados are very healthy. They pack many vitamins and minerals like potassium. Moreover, avocados are shown to assist the body to enter ketosis faster.

Meat and Poultry

These two are the staple food in most keto diets. Most of the keto meals revolve around using these two ingredients. Often this is because they contain no carbs and pack many vitamins and minerals. Moreover, they're an excellent source of protein.

Plain Greek Yogurt and pot cheese

These two food items are rich in protein and a small number of carbs, sufficiently small that you simply can safely include them into your keto diet. They also help suppress your appetite by making you are feeling full for extended and that they are often eaten alone and are still delicious.

Olive Oil

Olive oil is extremely beneficial for your heart because it contains monounsaturated fatty acid that helps decrease heart condition risk factors. Extra-virgin vegetable oil is additionally rich in antioxidants. The simplest thing is that vegetable oil is often used as a primary source of fat, and it's no carbs. An equivalent goes for olive.

Nuts and Seeds

These also are low in carbs but rich in fat. They're also healthy and have tons of nutrients and fiber. They assist in reducing heart conditions, cancer, depression, and other risks of diseases. The fiber in these also helps cause you to feel full for extended, so you'd consume fewer calories, and your body would spend more calories digesting them.

Berries

Many fruits pack too many carbs that make them unsuitable during a keto diet, but not berries. They're low in carbs and high in fiber. Many of the simplest berries to incorporate in your diet are blackberries, blueberries, raspberries, and strawberries.

Butter and Cream

These two food items pack many fats and a really bit of carbs, making them a natural choice to include in your keto diet.

Shirataki Noodles

If you're keen on noodles and pasta but don't want to offer abreast, then shirataki noodles are the right alternative. They're rich in water content and pack tons of fiber, which means low carbs and calories and hunger suppression.

Unsweetened Coffee and Tea

These two drinks are carb-free, goodbye as you don't add sugar, milk, or the other sweeteners. Both contain caffeine that improves your metabolism and suppresses your appetite. A word of warning to those that love light coffee and tea lattes, though. They're made with non-fat milk and contain tons of carbs.

Dark Chocolate and chocolate

These two food items are delicious and contain antioxidants. Bittersweet chocolate is related to the reduction of heart condition risk by lowering the vital sign. Just confirm that you simply choose only bittersweet chocolate with a minimum of 70% cocoa solids.

CHAPTER 3:

Foods to Avoid

In this chapter, I will show you the sorts of food you would like to avoid in the least costs. Because keto may be a keto diet, meaning you would like to prevent high-carbs food. Several foods you avoid is even healthy, but they only contain too many carbs. Here may be a list of typical food you ought to limit or avoid altogether.

Bread and Grains

Bread is a staple food in many countries. You've got loaves, bagels, tortillas, and the list goes on. However, regardless of what form bread takes, they still pack tons of carbs. An equivalent applies to whole-grain also because they're made up of refined flour.

Depending on your daily carb limit, eating a sandwich or bagel can put you over your daily limit. So, if you want to eat bread, it's best to form keto variants reception instead.

Grains like rice, wheat, and oats pack tons of carbs also. So, limit or avoid that too.

Fruits

Fruits are healthy for you. They need been linked to a lower risk of heart condition and cancer. However, there are a couple of that you simply got to avoid in your keto diets. The matter is that many of those foods pack quite a lot of carbs like banana, raisins, dates, mango, and pear.

As a general rule, avoid sweet and dried fruits. Berries are an exception because they are doing not contain the maximum amount of sugar and are rich in fiber. So, you'll still eat a number of them, around 50 grams. Moderation is vital.

Vegetables

Vegetables are even as healthy for your body. Most of the keto diet doesn't care what percentage of vegetables you eat goodbye as they're low in starch. Vegetables that are rich in fiber can help with weight loss. For one, they create you are feeling full for extended so that they help suppress your appetite. Another benefit is that your body would burn more calories to interrupt and digest them. Moreover, they assist control blood glucose and aid together with your bowel movements.

But that also means you would like to avoid or limit vegetables high in starch because they need more carbs than fiber. That has corn, potato, sweet potato, and beets.

Pasta

Pasta is additionally a staple food in many countries. It's versatile and convenient. Like the other suitable food, pasta is rich in carbs. So, once you are on your keto diet, spaghetti or the different sorts of pasta aren't recommended. You'll probably escape with it by eating a little portion, but that's impossible.

Thankfully, that doesn't mean you would like to offer abreast of it altogether. If you're craving pasta, you'll try other low-in carbs like spiralized veggies or shirataki noodles.

Cereal

Cereal is additionally an enormous offender because sugary breakfast cereals pack tons of carbs. That also applies to "healthy cereals." Simply because they use other words to explain their product doesn't mean that you simply should believe them. That also applies to oatmeal, whole-grain cereals, etc.

So, once you eat a bowl of cereal once you do keto, you're already over your carb limit, and that we haven't even added milk into the equation! Therefore, avoid whole-grain cereal or cereals that we mention here altogether.

Beer

In reality, you'll drink most alcoholic beverages carefully without worrying . as an example, dry wine doesn't have that a lot of carbs and liquor has no carbs in the least. So, you'll drink them without worry. Beer is an exception to the present rule because it packs tons of carbs.

Carbs in beers or other liquid are considered liquid carbs, and that they are even more dangerous than solid carbs. You see, once you eat food that's rich in carbs, you a minimum of feeling full. Once you drink liquid carbs, you are doing not feel full as quickly; therefore, the appetite suppression effect is small.

Sweetened Yogurt

Yogurt is very healthy because it's tasty and doesn't have that a lot of carbs. It's a versatile food to possess in your keto diet. The matter comes once you consume yogurt variants rich in carbs like fruit-flavored, low-fat, sweetened, or nonfat yogurt. One serving of sweetened yogurt contains as many carbs as one serving of dessert.

If you love yogurt, you'll escape with half a cup of plain Greek yogurt with 50 grams of raspberries or blackberries.

Juice

Fruit juices are perhaps the worst beverage you'll put into your system once you are on a keto diet. One may argue that drink provides some nutrients, but the matter is that it contains tons of carbs that are very easy to digest. As a result, your blood glucose level will spike whenever you drink it. That also applies to vegetable juice due to the fast-digesting carbs present.

Another problem is that the brain doesn't identically process liquid carbs as solid carbs. These carbs can help suppress appetite, but liquid carbs will only put your desire into overdrive.

Low-fat and fat-free salad dressings

As mentioned previously, fruits and vegetables are mainly okay as they're low in carbs. But if you've got to shop for salads, confine mind that commercial dressings pack more carbs than you think that, especially the fat-free and low-fat variants.

So, if you would like to enjoy your salad, dress your salad using creamy, full-fat dressing instead. To hamper on carbs, you'll use vinegar and vegetable oil, both of which are proven to assist with heart health and aid in weight loss.

Beans and Legumes

These also are very nutritious as they're rich in fiber. Research has shown that eating these have many health benefits like reduced inflammation and heart condition risk.

However, they're also rich in carbs. You'll be ready to enjoy a little amount of them once you are on your keto diet, but confirm you exactly recognize what proportion you'll eat before you exceed your carb limit.

Sugar

We mean sugar in any form, including honey. You'll already remember what foods that contain much sugar like cookies, candies, and cake are forbidden on a keto diet or the other sort of diet that's designed to reduce.

What you'll not remember is that nature's sugar, like honey, is simply as rich in carbs as processed sugar. Natural sorts of sugar contain even more carbs.

Not only that, sugar, generally, is rich in carbs, they also add little to no nutritional value to your meal. Once you are on a keto diet, you would like to stay in mind that your diet goes to contains food that's rich in fiber and nutritious. So, sugar is out of the question.

If you want to sweeten your food, you'll just use a healthy sweetener instead because they do not add as many carbs to your food.

Chips and Crackers

These two are a number of the foremost popular snacks. What some people didn't realize is that one packet of chips contain several servings and will not be all eaten in one go. The carbs can add up very quickly if you are doing not watch what you eat.

Crackers also pack tons of carbs, although the quantity varies supported how they're made. But even wholewheat crackers contain tons of carbs.

Due to how processed snacks are produced, it's difficult to prevent yourself from eating everything within a brief period of your time. Therefore, it's advised that you simply avoid them altogether.

Milk

Previously, I mentioned that cereal contains tons of carbs, and a breakfast cereal will put you over your carbs limit without you adding milk. Milk also has tons of carbs on its own. Therefore, avoid it if you'll albeit milk may be a good source of the many nutrients like calcium, potassium, and other B vitamins.

Of course, that doesn't mean that you simply need to ditch milk altogether. You'll escape with a tablespoon or two of milk for your coffee. But cream or half-and-half is best if you drink coffee frequently. These two contain only a few carbs. But if you're keen on drinking milk in large amounts or need it to form your favorite drinks, think about using coconut milk or unsweetened almond instead.

Gluten-free food

Wheat, barley, and rye all contain gluten. Some people that have disorder still want to enjoy these delicacies but unable to because their gut will become inflamed in response to gluten. As such, gluten-free variants are created to cater to their needs.

Gluten-free diets are very fashionable nowadays, but what many of us don't seem to understand is that they pack quite a lot of carbs. That has gluten-free bread, muffins, and other baked products. They contain even more carbs than their glutenous variant. Moreover, the flour wont to make these gluten-free products are made up of grains and starches so, once you consume a gluten-free bread, your blood glucose level spikes.

So, just stick with whole foods. Alternatively, you'll use almond or coconut flour to form your low-carb bread.

CHAPTER 4:

Breakfast Recipes

1. Cheese Crepes

Preparation time: 15 minutes

Cooking time: 20 minutes

Servings: 5

Ingredients:

- 6 ounces cream cheese
- 1/3 cup Parmesan cheese
- 6 large organic eggs
- 1 teaspoon granulated erythritol
- 1 1/2 tablespoon coconut flour
- 1/8 teaspoon xanthan gum
- 2 tablespoons unsalted butter

Directions:

1. Pulse the cream cheese, Parmesan cheese, eggs, and erythritol using a blender.
2. Place the coconut flour and xanthan gum and pulse again.
3. Now, pulse on medium speed. Transfer and put aside within 5 minutes.
4. Melt butter over medium-low heat.

5. Place 1 portion of the mixture and tilt the pan to spread into a thin layer.
6. Cook within 1½ minutes.
7. Flip the crepe and cook within 15-20 seconds more. Serve.

Nutrition:

Calories 297

Net Carbs 1.9 g

Total Fat 25.1 g

Cholesterol 281 mg

Total Carbs 3.5 g

Protein 13.7 g

2. Ricotta Pancakes

Preparation time: 10 minutes

Cooking time: 20 minutes

Servings: 4

Ingredients:

- 4 organic eggs

- ½ cup ricotta cheese
- ¼ cup vanilla whey protein powder
- ½ teaspoon organic baking powder
- salt
- ½ teaspoon liquid stevia
- 2 tablespoons unsalted butter

Directions:

1. Pulse all the fixing in the blender. Warm-up butter over medium heat. Put the batter and spread it evenly.
2. Cook within 2 minutes. Flip and cook again within 1–2 minutes. Serve.

Nutrition:

Calories 184

Net Carbs 2.7 g

Total Fat 12.9 g

Total Carbs 2.7 g

Sugar 0.8 g

Protein 14.6 g

3. Yogurt Waffles

Preparation time: 15 minutes

Cooking time: 25 minutes

Servings: 5

Ingredients:

- ½ cup golden flax seeds meal
- ½ cup plus 3 tablespoons almond flour
- 1-1½ tablespoons granulated erythritol
- 1 tablespoon vanilla whey protein powder
- ¼ teaspoon baking soda
- ½ teaspoon organic baking powder
- ¼ teaspoon xanthan gum
- Salt
- 1 large organic egg
- 1 organic egg
- 2 tablespoons unsweetened almond milk
- 1½ tablespoons unsalted butter
- 3 ounces plain Greek yogurt

Directions:

1. Preheat the waffle iron and then grease it.
2. Mix add the flour, erythritol, protein powder, baking soda, baking powder, xanthan gum, and salt.
3. Beat the egg white until stiff peaks. In a third bowl, add 2 egg yolks, whole egg, almond milk, butter, and yogurt, and beat.
4. Put egg mixture into the bowl of the flour mixture and mix.
5. Gently, fold in the beaten egg whites. Place ¼ cup of the mixture into preheated waffle iron and cook for about 4–5 minutes. Serve.

Nutrition:

Calories 250

Net Carbs 3.2 g

Total Fat 18.7 g

Protein 8.4 g

4. Broccoli Muffins

Preparation time: 15 minutes

Cooking time: 20 minutes

Servings: 6

Ingredients:

- 2 tablespoons unsalted butter
- 6 large organic eggs
- ½ cup heavy whipping cream
- ½ cup Parmesan cheese
- Salt & ground black pepper
- 1¼ cups broccoli
- 2 tablespoons parsley
- ½ cup Swiss cheese

Directions:

1. Warm-up oven to 350°F, then grease a 12-cup muffin tin.
2. Mix the eggs, cream, Parmesan cheese, salt, and black pepper.
3. Divide the broccoli and parsley in the muffin cup.
4. Top with the egg mixture, with Swiss cheese.
5. Bake within 20 minutes. Cool for about 5 minutes. Serve.

Nutrition:

Calories 231

Net Carbs 2 g

Total Fat 18.1 g

Cholesterol 228 mg

Sodium 352 mg

Protein 13.5 g

5. Pumpkin Bread

Preparation time: 15 minutes

Cooking time: 1 hour

Servings: 16

Ingredients:

- 1 2/3 cups almond flour
- 1½ teaspoons organic baking powder
- ½ teaspoon pumpkin pie spice
- ½ teaspoon cinnamon
- ½ teaspoon cloves
- ½ teaspoon salt
- 8 ounces cream cheese
- 6 organic eggs
- 1 tablespoon coconut flour
- 1 cup powdered erythritol
- 1 teaspoon stevia powder
- 1 teaspoon organic lemon extract
- 1 cup pumpkin puree
- ½ cup of coconut oil

Directions:

1. Warm-up oven to 325°F. Grease 2 bread loaf pans.
2. Mix almond flour, baking powder, spices, and salt in a small bowl.

3. In a second bowl, add the cream cheese, 1 egg, coconut flour, ¼ cup of erythritol, and ¼ teaspoon of the stevia, and beat.

4. In a third bowl, add the pumpkin puree, oil, 5 eggs, ¾ cup of the erythritol, and ¾ teaspoon of the stevia and mix.

5. Mix the pumpkin mixture into the bowl of the flour mixture.

6. Place about ¼ of the pumpkin mixture into each loaf pan.

7. Top each pan with the cream cheese mixture, plus the rest pumpkin mixture.

8. Bake within 50–60 minutes. Cold within 10 minutes. Slice and serve.

Nutrition:

Calories 216

Net Carbs 2.5 g

Total Fat 19.8 g

Cholesterol 77 mg

Sodium 140 mg

Protein 3.4 g

- Ground black pepper
- 4 tablespoons cheddar cheese
- 2 cooked bacon
- 1 tablespoon scallion greens

Directions:

1. Warm-up oven to 400°F. Remove 2 tablespoons of flesh from the avocado.

2. Place avocado halves into a small baking dish.

3. Crack an egg in each avocado half and sprinkle with salt plus black pepper.

4. Top each egg with cheddar cheese evenly.

5. Bake within 20 minutes. Serve with bacon and chives.

Nutrition:

Calories 343 Net Carbs 2.2 g

Total Fat 29.1 g

Cholesterol 186 mg

Sodium 372 mg

Protein 13.8 g

6. Eggs in Avocado Cups

Preparation time: 10 minutes

Cooking time: 20 minutes

Servings: 4

Ingredients:

- 2 avocados
- 4 organic eggs
- Salt

7. Cheddar Scramble

Preparation time: 10 minutes

Cooking time: 8 minutes

Servings: 6

Ingredients:

- 2 tablespoons olive oil
- 1 small yellow onion

- 12 large organic eggs
- Salt and ground black pepper
- 4 ounces cheddar cheese

Directions;

1. Warm-up oil over medium heat.
2. Sauté the onion within 4–5 minutes.
3. Add the eggs, salt, and black pepper and cook within 3 minutes.
4. Remove then stir in the cheese. Serve.

Nutrition:

Calories 264

Net Carbs 1.8 g

Total Fat 20.9 g

Cholesterol 392 mg

Sodium 285 mg

Protein 17.4 g

8. Bacon Omelet

Preparation time: 10 minutes

Cooking time: 15 minutes

Servings: 2

Ingredients:

- 4 organic eggs
- 1 tablespoon chives
- Salt
- ground black pepper
- 4 bacon slices

- 1 tablespoon unsalted butter
- 2 ounces cheddar cheese

Directions:

1. Beat the eggs, chives, salt, and black pepper in a bowl.
2. Warm-up a pan over medium-high heat then cooks the bacon slices within 8–10 minutes.
3. Chop the bacon slices. Melt butter and cook the egg mixture within 2 minutes.
4. Flip the omelet and top with chopped bacon. Cook within 1–2 minutes.
5. Remove then put the cheese in the center of the omelet. Serve.

Nutrition:

Calories 427

Net Carbs 1.2 g

Total Fat 28.2 g

Cholesterol 469 mg

Sodium 668 mg

Sugar 1 g

Protein 29.1 g

9. Green Veggies Quiche

Preparation time: 20 minutes

Cooking time: 20 minutes

Servings: 4

Ingredients:

- 6 organic eggs
- ½ cup unsweetened almond milk

- Salt and ground black pepper
- 2 cups baby spinach
- ½ cup green bell pepper
- 1 scallion
- ¼ cup cilantro
- 1 tablespoon chives,
- 3 tablespoons mozzarella cheese

Directions:

1. Warm-up oven to 400°F.
2. Grease a pie dish. Beat eggs, almond milk, salt, and black pepper. Set aside.
3. In another bowl, add the vegetables and herbs then mix.
4. Place the veggie mixture and top with the egg mixture in the pie dish.
5. Bake within 20 minutes. Remove then sprinkle with the Parmesan cheese.
6. Slice and serve.

Nutrition:

Calories 176

Net Carbs 4.1 g

Total Fat 10.9 g

Cholesterol 257 mg

Sugar 4 g

Protein 15.4 g

10. Chicken & Asparagus Frittata

Preparation time: 15 minutes

Cooking time: 12 minutes

Servings: 4

Ingredients:

- ½ cup grass-fed chicken breast
- 1/3 cup Parmesan cheese
- 6 organic eggs
- Salt
- ground black pepper
- 1/3 cup boiled asparagus
- ¼ cup cherry tomatoes
- ¼ cup mozzarella cheese

Directions:

1. Warm-up broiler of the oven, then mix Parmesan cheese, eggs, salt, and black pepper in a bowl.
2. Melt butter, then cooks the chicken and asparagus within 2–3 minutes.
3. Add the egg mixture and tomatoes and mix. Cook within 4–5 minutes.
4. Remove then sprinkle with the Parmesan cheese.
5. Transfer the wok under the broiler and broil within 3–4 minutes. Slice and serve.

Nutrition:

Calories 158

Net Carbs 1.3 g

Total Fat 9.3 g

Cholesterol 265 mg

Sodium 267 mg

Sugar 1 g

11. Southwest Scrambled Egg Bites

Preparation time: 10 minutes

Cooking time: 23 minutes

Servings: 4

Ingredients:

- 5 eggs
- 1/2 teaspoon hot pepper sauce
- 1/3 cup tomatoes
- 3 tablespoons green chilies
- 1 teaspoon black pepper
- 1/2 teaspoon salt
- 2 tablespoons nondairy milk

Directions:

1. Mix both the eggs and milk in a large cup. Add the hot sauce, pepper, and salt. Put a small diced chilies and diced tomatoes in silicone cups.

2. Fill each with 3/4 full with the egg mixture.

3. Put the trivet in the pot and pour 1 cup water. Put the mold on the trivet. Set to high for 8 minutes. Cool down before serving.

Nutrition:

Calories: 106 Carbs: 2g Protein: 7.5g

Fats: 7.4g

12. Omelet Bites

Preparation time: 5 minutes

Cooking time: 8 minutes

Servings: 3

Ingredients:

- 1 handful mushrooms
- green onion
- green peppers
- 1/8 teaspoon hot sauce
- Pepper, salt, mustard, garlic powder
- 1/2 cup cheese cheddar
- 1/2 cup cheese cottage
- 2 deli ham slices
- 4 eggs

Directions:

1. Whisk eggs, then the cheddar and cottage. Put the ham, veggies, and seasonings; mix. Pour the mixture into greased silicone molds.

2. Put the trivet with the molds in the pot then fill with 2 cups water. Steam for about 8 minutes.

Nutrition:

Calories: 260

Carbs: 6g

Protein: 22g

Fats: 16g

13. Avocado Pico Egg Bites

Preparation time: 15 minutes

Cooking time: 10 minutes

Servings: 7

Ingredients:

- Egg bites:
- 1/ cup cheese cottage
- 1/2 cup cheese Mexican blend
- 1/4 cup cream heavy cream
- 1/4 teaspoon chili powder
- 1/4 teaspoon cumin
- 1/4 teaspoon garlic powder
- 4 eggs
- Pepper
- salt
- Pico de Gallo:
- 1 avocado
- 1 jalapeno
- 1/2 teaspoon salt
- 1/4 onion
- 2 tablespoons cilantro
- 2 teaspoons lime juice
- 4 Roma tomatoes

Directions:

1. Mix all of the Pico de Gallo fixing except for the avocado. Gently fold in the avocado.
2. Blend all the egg bites ingredients in a blender. Spoon 1 tablespoon of Pico de Gallo into each egg bite silicone mold.
3. Place the trivet in the pot then fill with 1 cup water. Put the molds in the trivet. Set to high within 10 minutes. Remove. Serve topped with cheese and Pico de Gallo.

Nutrition:

Calories: 118 Carbs: 1g Protein: 7g Fats: 9g

14. Salmon Scramble

Preparation time: 10 minutes

Cooking time: 5 minutes

Servings: 1

Ingredients:

- 2 smoked salmon pieces
- 1 organic egg yolk
- 1/8 teaspoon. red pepper flakes
- Black pepper
- 2 organic eggs
- 1 tablespoon. dill
- 1/8 teaspoon. garlic powder
- 1 tablespoon. olive oil

Directions:

1. Beat all items except salmon and oil. Stir in chopped salmon. Warm-up oil over medium-low heat in a frying pan. Add the egg mixture and cook within 3-5 minutes. Serve.

Nutrition:

Calories: 376

Carbs: 3.4g

Protein: 24g

Fats: 24.8g

15. Cheddar & Bacon Egg Bites

Preparation time: 10 minutes

Cooking time: 8 minutes

Servings: 7

Ingredients:

- 1 cup sharp cheddar cheese
- 1 tablespoon parsley flakes
- 4 eggs
- 4 tablespoons cream
- Hot sauce
- 1 cup of water
- 1/2 cup cheese
- 4 slices bacon

Directions:

1. Blend the cream, cheddar, cottage, and egg in the blender; 30 seconds. Stir in the parsley. Grease silicone egg bite molds.

2. Divide the crumbled bacon between them. Put the egg batter into each cup. With a piece of foil, cover each mold.

3. Place the trivet with the molds in the pot then fill with 1 cup water. Steam for 8 minutes. Remove, let rest for 5 minutes.

4. Serve, sprinkled with black pepper and optional hot sauce.

Nutrition:

Calories: 167

Carbs: 1.5g

Protein: 13.5g

Fats: 11.7g

16. Mexican Scrambled Eggs

Preparation time: 5 minutes

Cooking time: 10 minutes

Servings: 6

Ingredients:

- 6 Eggs
- 2 Jalapeños
- 1 Tomato
- 3 oz. Cheese
- 2 tablespoon. Butter

Directions:

1. Warm-up butter over medium heat in a large pan. Add tomatoes, jalapeños, and green onions then cook within 3 minutes.

2. Add eggs, and continue within 2 minutes. Add cheese and season to taste. Serve.

Nutrition:

Calories: 239

Carbs: 2.38g

Protein: 13.92g

Fats: 19.32g

17. Bacon Egg Bites

Preparation time: 10 minutes

Cooking time: 22 minutes

Servings: 9

Ingredients:

- 1 cup cheese
- 1/2 green pepper
- 1/2 cup cottage cheese
- 4 slices bacon
- Pepper
- salt
- 1 cup red onion
- 1 cup of water
- 1/4 cup whip cream
- 1/4 cup egg whites
- 4 eggs

Directions:

1. Blend egg whites, eggs, cream, cheese (cottage), shredded cheese, pepper, and salt within 30 to 45 seconds in a blender.

Put the egg mixture into mini muffin cups.

2. Top each with bacon, peppers, and onion. Cover the muffin cups tightly with foil. Place the trivet in the pot and pour 1 cup water.

3. Put the cups on the trivet. Set to steam for 12 minutes.

Nutrition:

Calories: 124

Carbs: 3g

Protein: 9g

Fats: 8

18. Caprese Omelet

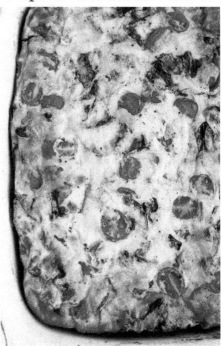

Preparation time: 10 minutes

Cooking time: 10 minutes

Servings: 2

Ingredients:

- 6 eggs
- Olive oil 2 tablespoon.
- Halved cherry tomatoes 3½ oz.

- Dried basil 1 tablespoon.
- Mozzarella cheese 5 1/3 oz.

Directions:

1. Mix the basil, eggs, salt and black pepper in a bowl. Place a large skillet with oil over medium heat. Once hot, add tomatoes and cook.

2. Top with egg and cook. Add cheese, adjust heat to low, and allow to set before serving fully.

Nutrition:

Calories: 423

Carbs: 6.81g Protein: 43.08g

Fats: 60.44g

19. Sausage Omelet

Preparation time: 10 minutes

Cooking time: 15 minutes

Servings: 2

Ingredients:

- ½ pound gluten-free sausage links
- ½ cup heavy whipping cream
- Salt
- black pepper
- 8 large organic eggs
- 1 cup cheddar cheese
- ¼ teaspoon. red pepper flakes

Directions:

1. Warm-up oven to 350°F. Grease a baking dish. Cook the sausage within 8–10 minutes.

2. Put the rest of the fixing in a bowl and beat. Remove sausage from the heat.

3. Place cooked sausage in the baking dish then top with the egg mixture. Bake within 30 minutes. Slice and serve.

Nutrition:

Calories: 334

Carbs: 1.1g

Protein: 20.6g

Fats: 27.3g

20. Brown Hash with Zucchini

Preparation time: 10 minutes

Cooking time: 20 minutes

Servings: 2

Ingredients:

- 1 small onion
- 6 to 8 mushrooms
- 2 Cups grass-fed ground beef
- 1 Pinch salt
- 1 Pinch ground black pepper
- ½ teaspoon smoked paprika
- 2 eggs
- 1 avocado
- 10 black olives

Directions:

1. Warm-up air fryer for 350° F. Grease a pan with coconut oil. Add the onions, the mushrooms, the salt plus pepper to the pan.

2. Add the ground beef and the smoked paprika and eggs. Mix, then place the pan

in Air Fryer. Set to cook within 18 to 20 minutes with a temperature, 375° F.

3. Serve with chopped parsley and diced avocado!

Nutrition:

Calories: 290

Carbs: 15g

Protein: 20g

Fats: 23g

CHAPTER 5:

Lunch Recipes

21. Easy Keto Smoked Salmon Lunch Bowl.

Preparation time: 15 minutes

Cooking time: 0 minutes

Servings: 2

Ingredients:

- Twelve-ounce smoked salmon
- 4 tablespoon mayonnaise
- Two-ounce spinach
- One tablespoon olive oil
- One medium lime
- Pepper
- Salt

Directions:

1. Arrange the mayonnaise, salmon, spinach on a plate. Sprinkle olive oil over the spinach.
2. Serve with lime wedges and put salt plus pepper.

Nutrition:

457 calories

1.9g net carbs

34.8g fats

32.3g protein.

22. Easy One-Pan Ground Beef and Green Beans

Preparation time: 15 minutes

Cooking time: 15 minutes

Servings: 2

Ingredients:

- Ten ounces ground beef
- Nine ounces green beans
- Pepper
- salt
- Two tablespoons sour cream
- 3½ ounces butter

Directions:

1. Warm-up the butter to a pan over high heat.

2. Put the ground beef plus the pepper and salt. Cook.

3. Reduce heat to medium. Add the remaining butter and the green beans then cook within five minutes. Put pepper and salt, then transfer. Serve with a dollop of sour cream.

Nutrition:

6.65g Net Carbs 787.5 Calories

71.75g Fats 27.5g Protein.

23. Easy Spinach and Bacon Salad

Preparation time: 15 minutes

Cooking time: 15 minutes

Servings: 4

Ingredients:

- Eight ounces spinach
- Four large hard-boiled eggs
- 6 ounces bacon
- Two medium red onion
- Two cup mayonnaise
- Pepper
- salt

Directions:

1. Cook the bacon, then chop into pieces, set aside.

2. Slice the hard-boiled eggs, and then rinse the spinach.

3. Combine the lettuce, mayonnaise, and bacon fat into a large cup, put pepper and salt.

4. Add the red onion, sliced eggs, and bacon into the salad, then toss. Serve.

Nutrition:

45.9g Fats 509.15 Calories 2.5g Net Carbs

19.75g protein

24. Easy Keto Italian Plate

Preparation time: 15 minutes

Cooking time: 0 minutes

Servings: 2

Ingredients:

- Seven ounces mozzarella cheese
- Seven ounces prosciutto
- Two tomatoes
- Four tablespoons olive oil
- Ten whole green olives
- Pepper
- salt

Directions:

1. Arrange the tomato, olives, mozzarella, and prosciutto on a plate.

2. Season the tomato and cheese with pepper and salt. Serve with olive oil.

Nutrition:

780.98 Calories

5.9g Net Carbs

60.74g Fats

50.87g protein.

25. Fresh Broccoli and Dill Keto Salad

Preparation time: 15 minutes

Cooking time: 7 minutes

Servings: 3

Ingredients:

- 16 ounces broccoli
- One/Two cup mayonnaise
- 3/4 cup chopped dill
- Salt
- pepper

Directions:

1. Boil salted water in a saucepan. Put the chopped broccoli to the pot and boil for 3-5 minutes. Drain and set aside. Once cooled, mix the rest of the fixing. Put pepper and salt, then serve.

Nutrition:

303.33 Calories

6.2g Net Carbs

28.1g Fats

4.03g Protein.

26. Keto Smoked Salmon Filled Avocados.

Preparation time: 15 minutes

Cooking time: 0 minutes

Servings: 1

Ingredients:

- One avocado
- Three ounces smoked salmon
- Four tablespoons sour cream
- One tablespoon lemon juice
- Pepper
- salt

Directions:

1. Cut the avocado into two. Place the sour cream in the hollow parts of the avocado with smoked salmon. Put pepper and salt, squeeze lemon juice over the top. Serve.

Nutrition:

517 Calories

6.7g Net Carbs

42.6g Fats

20.6g Protein

27. Low-Carb Broccoli Lemon Parmesan Soup

Preparation time: 15 minutes

Cooking time: 15 minutes

Servings: 4

Ingredients:

- Three cups of water
- One cup unsweetened almond milk
- Thirty-two ounces broccoli florets
- One cup heavy whipping cream
- 3/4 cup Parmesan cheese
- Salt
- pepper
- Two tablespoons lemon juice

Directions:

1. Cook broccoli plus water over medium-high heat.
2. Take out 1 cup of the cooking liquid, and remove the rest.
3. Blend half the broccoli, reserved cooking oil, unsweetened almond milk, heavy cream, and salt plus pepper in a blender.
4. Put the blended items to the remaining broccoli, and stir with Parmesan cheese and lemon juice. Cook until heated through. Serve with Parmesan cheese on the top.

Nutrition:

371 Calories

11.67g Net Carbs

28.38g Fats

14.63g Protein

28. Prosciutto and Mozzarella Bomb

Preparation time: 15 minutes

Cooking time: 10 minutes

Servings: 4

Ingredients:

- Four ounces sliced prosciutto
- Eight ounces mozzarella ball
- Olive oil

Directions:

1. Layer half of the prosciutto vertically. Lay the remaining slices horizontally across the first set of slices. Place mozzarella ball, upside down, onto the crisscrossed prosciutto slices.
2. Wrap the mozzarella ball with the prosciutto slices. Warm-up the olive oil in a skillet, crisp the prosciutto, then serve.

Nutrition:

253 Calories

1.08g Net Carbs

19.35g Fats

18g Protein

29. Summer Tuna Avocado Salad

Preparation time: 15 minutes

Cooking time: 0 minutes

Servings: 2

Ingredients:

- 1can tuna flake
- One medium avocado
- One medium English cucumber
- ¼ cup cilantro
- One tablespoon lemon juice
- One tablespoon olive oil
- Pepper
- salt

Directions:

1. Put the first 4 ingredients into a salad bowl. Sprinkle with the lemon and olive oil. Serve.

Nutrition:

303 Calories

5.2g Net Carbs

22.6g Fats

16.7g Protein.

30. Mushrooms & Goat Cheese Salad

Preparation time: 15 minutes

Cooking time: 10 minutes

Servings: 1

Ingredients:

- One tablespoon butter
- Two ounces cremini mushrooms
- Pepper
- salt
- Four ounces spring mix
- One-ounce cooked bacon
- One-ounce goat cheese
- One tablespoon olive oil
- One tablespoon balsamic vinegar

Directions:

1. Sautee the mushrooms, put pepper and salt.
2. Place the salad greens in a bowl. Top with goat cheese and crumbled bacon.
3. Mix these in the salad once the mushrooms are done.
4. Whisk the olive oil in a small bowl and balsamic vinegar. Put the salad on top and serve.

Nutrition:

243 Cal 21 gram total fat 8 gram carb

4 gram saturated fat1 gram fiber

31. Keto Chicken Club Lettuce Wrap

Preparation Time: 15 minutes

Cooking Time: 15 minutes

Servings: 1

Ingredients:

- 1 head iceberg lettuce
- 1 tablespoon. mayonnaise
- 6 slices of organic chicken
- Bacon
- Tomato

Directions:

1. Layer 6-8 large leaves of lettuce in the center of the parchment paper, around 9-10 inches.
2. Spread the mayo in the center and lay with chicken, bacon, and tomato.
3. Roll the wrap halfway through, then roll tuck in the ends of the wrap.
4. Cut it in half. Serve.

Nutrition:

Net carbs: 4g

Fiber: 2g

Fat: 78g

Protein: 28g

Calories: 837

32. Keto Broccoli Salad

Preparation Time: 10 minutes

Cooking Time: 0 minutes

Servings: 4-6

Ingredients:

For salad

- 2 Broccoli
- 2 Red Cabbage
- .5 c Sliced Almonds
- 1 Green Onions
- .5 c Raisins

For the orange almond dressing

- .33 c Orange Juice
- .25 c Almond Butter
- 2 tablespoon Coconut Aminos
- 1 Shallot
- Salt

Directions:

1. Pulse the salt, shallot, amino, nut butter, and orange juice using a blender.
2. Combine other fixing in a bowl. Toss it with dressing and serve.

Nutrition:

Net carbs: 13g Fiber: 0g Fat: 94g Protein: 22g

Calories: 1022

33. Keto Sheet Pan Chicken and Rainbow Veggies

Preparation Time: 15 minutes

Cooking Time: 25 minutes

Servings: 4

Ingredients:

- Nonstick spray
- 1-pound Chicken Breasts
- 1 tablespoon Sesame Oil
- 2 tablespoon Soy Sauce
- 2 tablespoon Honey
- 2 Red Pepper
- 2 Yellow Pepper
- 3 Carrots
- ½ Broccoli
- 2 Red Onions
- 2 tablespoon EVOO
- Pepper & salt
- .25 c Parsley

Directions:

1. Grease the baking sheet, warm-up the oven to a temperature of 400-degrees.
2. Put the chicken in the middle of the sheet. Separately, combine the oil and the soy sauce. Brush over the chicken.
3. Separate veggies across the plate. Sprinkle with oil and then toss. Put pepper & salt.

4. Set tray into the oven and cook within 25 minutes. Garnish using parsley. Serve.

Nutrition:

Net carbs: 9g

Fiber: 0g

Fat: 30g

Protein: 30g

Calories: 437kcal

34. Cole Slaw Keto Wrap

Preparation Time: 15 minutes

Cooking Time: 0 minutes

Servings: 2

Ingredients:

- 3 c Red Cabbage
- .5 c Green Onions
- .75 c Mayo
- 2 teaspoon Apple Cider Vinegar
- .25 teaspoon Salt
- 16 pcs Collard Green
- 1-pound Ground Meat, cooked
- .33 c Alfalfa Sprouts
- Toothpicks

Directions:

1. Mix slaw items with a spoon in a large-sized bowl.

2. Place a collard green on a plate and scoop a tablespoon of coleslaw on the edge of the leaf. Top it with a scoop of meat and sprouts. Roll and tuck the sides.

3. Insert the toothpicks. Serve.

Nutrition:

Calories: 409

Net carbs: 4g

Fiber: 2g

Fat: 42g

Protein: 2g

35. Keto Caesar Salad

Preparation Time: 15 minutes

Cooking Time: 0 minutes

Servings: 4

Ingredients:

- Cups Mayonnaise
- 3 tablespoons Apple Cider Vinegar
- 1 teaspoon Dijon Mustard
- 4 Anchovy Fillets
- 24 Romaine Heart Leaves
- 4 oz Pork Rinds
- Parmesan

Directions:

1. Process the mayo with ACV, mustard, and anchovies into a blender. Prepare romaine leaves and pour the dressing. Top with pork rinds and serve.

Nutrition:

Net carbs: 4g Fiber: 3g

Fat: 86g Protein: 47g

Calories: 993kcal

36. Skinny Bang-Bang Zucchini Noodles

Preparation Time: 15 minutes

Cooking Time: 15 minutes

Servings: 4

Ingredients:

For the noodles

- 4 medium zucchinis spiraled
- 1 tablespoon. olive oil

For the sauce

- 0.25 cup + 2 tablespoons Plain Greek Yogurt
- 0.25 cup + 2 tablespoons Mayo
- 0.25 cup + 2 tablespoons Thai Sweet Chili Sauce
- Teaspoons Honey
- Teaspoons Sriracha
- 2 teaspoons Lime Juice

Directions:

1. Pour the oil into a large skillet at medium temperature. Stir in the spiraled zucchini noodles. Cook.

2. Remove then drain, and let it rest 10 minutes. Combine sauce items into a bowl.

3. Mix in the noodles to the sauce. Serve.

Nutrition:

Net carbs: 18g

Fiber: 0g

Fat: 1g

Protein: 9g

Calories: 161g

37. Keto Bacon Sushi

Preparation time: 15 minutes

Cooking time: 13 minutes

Servings: 4

Ingredients:

- Six slices bacon
- One avocado
- Two Persian cucumbers
- Two medium carrots
- Four oz. cream cheese

Directions:

1. Warm-up oven to 400F. Line a baking sheet. Place bacon halves in an even layer and bake, 11 to 13 minutes.

2. Meanwhile, slice cucumbers, avocado, and carrots into parts roughly the width of the bacon.

3. Spread an even layer of cream cheese in the cooled down bacon. Divide vegetables evenly and place it on one end. Roll up vegetables tightly. Garnish and serve.

Nutrition:

11 g carbohydrates

28g protein

30g fat

38. Chicken Wings and Blue Cheese Dressing

Preparation Time: 70 minutes

Cooking Time: 25 minutes

Servings: 4

Ingredients:

- One-third cup mayonnaise
- One-fourth cup sour cream
- Three teaspoon. lemon juice
- One-fourth teaspoon. of each:
- Salt
- Garlic powder
- Half cup whipping cream
- Three ounces blue cheese

For the chicken wings:

- Two pounds chicken wings
- Two tablespoons. olive oil

- One-fourth teaspoon. garlic powder
- One clove garlic
- One-third teaspoon. black pepper
- One teaspoon. salt
- Two ounces parmesan cheese

Directions:

1. Mix all the blue cheese dressing items in a bowl. Chill within forty minutes.
2. Combine the chicken with olive oil and spices. Marinate for thirty minutes.
3. Bake in the oven for twenty-five minutes. Toss the chicken wings with parmesan cheese in a bowl.
4. Serve with blue cheese dressing by the side.

Nutrition:

Calories: 839.3

Protein: 51.2g

Carbs: 2.9g

Fat: 67.8g

Fiber: 0.2g

39. Salmon Burgers with Lemon Butter and Mash

Preparation Time: 70 minutes

Cooking Time: 15 minutes

Servings: 4

Ingredients:

For the salmon burgers:

- Two pounds salmon
- One egg
- Half yellow onion
- One teaspoon. salt
- Half teaspoon. black pepper
- Two ounces butter
- For the green mash:
- One-pound broccoli
- Five ounces of butter
- Two ounces parmesan cheese
- Pepper
- salt

For the lemon butter:

- Four ounces butter
- Two tablespoons. lemon juice
- Pepper
- salt

Directions:

1. Warm-up your oven at 100 degrees.
2. Cut the salmon into small pieces. Combine all the burger items with the fish in a blender. Pulse for thirty seconds. Make eight patties.
3. Warm-up butter in an iron skillet. Fry the burgers for five minutes.
4. Boil water, along with some salt in a pot, put the broccoli florets. Cook for three to four minutes. Drain. Add parmesan cheese and butter. Blend the ingredients using an immersion blender. Add pepper and salt.

5. Combine lemon juice with butter, pepper, and salt. Beat using an electric beater.

6. Put a dollop of lemon butter on the top and green mash by the side. Serve.

Nutrition:

Calories: 1025.3

Protein: 44.5g

Carbs: 6.8g

Fat: 90.1g

Fiber: 3.1g

40. Egg Salad Recipe

Preparation Time: 15 minutes

Cooking Time: 20 minutes

Servings: 6

Ingredients:

- 3 tablespoon. mayonnaise
- 3 tablespoon. Greek yogurt
- 2 tablespoon. red wine vinegar
- Kosher salt
- ground black pepper
- Eight hard-boiled eggs

- Eight strips bacon
- One avocado
- 1/2 c. crumbled blue cheese
- 1/2 c. cherry tomatoes
- 2 tablespoon. chives

Directions:

1. Stir mayonnaise, cream, and the red wine vinegar in a small bowl put pepper and salt.

2. Mix the eggs, bacon, avocado, blue cheese, and cherry tomatoes in a large bowl. Fold in the mayonnaise dressing put salt and pepper. Garnish with the chives and serve.

Nutrition:

Calories: 200

Carbs: 3g

Fat: 18g

Protein: 10g

41. Taco Stuffed Avocados

Preparation Time: 10 minutes

Cooking Time: 25 minutes

Servings: 8

Ingredients:

- Four ripe avocados

- Lime juice
- 1 tablespoon. extra-virgin olive oil
- One onion
- 1 lb. ground beef
- One packet taco seasoning
-      Kosher salt
- ground black pepper
- 2/3 c. Mexican cheese
- 1/2 c. lettuce
- 1/2 c. quartered grape tomatoes
- Sour cream

Directions:

1. Scoop a bit of avocado flesh. Put. Squeeze lime juice overall avocados.
2. Warm-up oil in a skillet over medium heat. Put onion, and cook within 5 minutes. Put ground beef and taco seasoning. Put salt and pepper, and cook within 6 minutes. Remove and drain.
3. Fill every half of the avocado with beef, then top with reserved avocado, cheese, lettuce, tomato, and a sour dollop cream. Serve.

Nutrition:

Calories: 324

Carbs: 16g

Fat: 24g

Protein: 15g

42. Buffalo Shrimp Lettuce Wraps

Preparation Time: 15 minutes

Cooking Time: 20 minutes

Servings: 4

Ingredients:

- 1/4 tablespoon. butter
- Two garlic cloves
- 1/4 c. hot sauce
- 1 tablespoon. extra-virgin olive oil
- 1 lb. shrimp tails removed
- Kosher salt
- ground black pepper
- One head romaine leaf
- 1/4 red onion
- One rib celery
- 1/2 c. blue cheese

Directions:

1. Make buffalo sauce:
2. Dissolve the butter over medium heat in a small saucepan. Put the garlic and cook for 1 minute. Put hot sauce, and stir. Adjust to low.
3. Make shrimp:
4. Warm-up oil in a large skillet over medium heat. Put shrimp, salt and pepper to season. Cook, around 2 minutes per side. Remove then put buffalo sauce, toss.
5. Assemble wraps:
6. Put a small scoop of shrimp to a roman leaf center, then top with red onion, celery, and blue cheese. Serve.

Nutrition:

Calories: 242

Carbs: 7g

Fat: 12g

Protein: 25g

43. Broccoli Bacon Salad

Preparation Time: 15 minutes

Cooking Time: 15 minutes

Servings: 6

Ingredients:

For the salad:

- kosher salt 3
- heads broccoli
- Two carrots
- 1/2 red onion
- 1/2 c. cranberries
- 1/2 c. almonds
- Six slices bacon
- For the dressing:
- 1/2 c. mayonnaise
- 3 tablespoon. apple cider vinegar
- kosher salt
- ground black pepper

Directions:

1. Boil 4 cups of salted water. Prepare a large bowl of ice water.

2. Put broccoli florets to the heated water, and cook within 1 to 2 minutes. Put the ice water in the prepared cup. Drain.

3. Combine broccoli, red onion, carrots, cranberries, nuts, and bacon in a large bowl.

4. Mix vinegar and mayonnaise in a bowl and put salt plus pepper.

5. Pour the broccoli mixture over the dressing. Mix and serve.

Nutrition:

Calories: 280

Carbs: 9g

Fat: 25g

Protein: 6g

44. Keto Egg Salad

Preparation Time: 15 minutes

Cooking Time: 15 minutes

Servings: 4

Ingredients:

- 3 tablespoon. mayonnaise
- 2 teaspoon. lemon juice
- 1 tablespoon. chives
- Ground black pepper

- Kosher salt
- Six hard-boiled eggs
- One avocado
- Lettuce
- Cooked bacon

Directions:

1. Mix the mayonnaise, lemon juice, and chives, put pepper and salt.
2. Add eggs and avocado to mix. Serve with Bacon and Lettuce.

Nutrition:

Calories: 408

Carbs: 5g

Fat: 39g

Protein: 13g

45. Keto Wrap

Preparation Time: 15 minutes

Cooking Time: 5 minutes

Servings: 5

Ingredients:

- 1 egg
- 0.5 teaspoon coconut fat
- 0.5 teaspoon curry powder

Directions:

1. Warm-up coconut fat in a small frying pan over high heat.
2. Beat the egg plus the curry powder with salt in a bowl.
3. Put the batter into the frying pan. Bake this wafer-thin omelet within 10-20 seconds.
4. Turn the wrap over and bake for a few seconds. Serve.

Nutrition:

Calories: 128 kcal

Protein: 6g

Fats: 12g

Fiber: 0.3 g

Carbohydrates: 1 g

46. Savory Keto Muffins

Preparation Time: 15 minutes

Cooking Time: 20 minutes

Servings: 5

Ingredients:

- 4 eggs
- 1 forest outing
- 100 grams chorizo
- 75 grams mascarpone
- 100 grams grated cheese
- Salt
- pepper

Directions:

1. Warm-up oven to 175° Celsius.
2. Beat the eggs with the mascarpone.
3. Add the spring onion, cheese, and chorizo to the egg batter. Put salt and pepper. Mix.
4. Bake within 9 - 14 minutes. Cool down and serve.

Nutrition:

Calories: 315 kcal

Protein: 17g

Fats: 26g

Fiber: 1g

Carbohydrates: 0g

47. Turkey and Cream Cheese Sauce

Preparation Time: 15 minutes

Cooking Time: 25 minutes

Servings: 5

Ingredients:

- Two tablespoons. butter
- Two pounds of turkey breast
- Two cups whipping cream
- Seven ounces cream cheese
- One tablespoon. tamari soy sauce
- Pepper
- salt
- -1- & 1/2-ounces capers

Directions:

1. Warm-up, the oven at 170 Celsius, then dissolve half butter in an iron skillet.
2. Rub the breast of turkey with pepper and salt. Fry within five minutes.
3. Bake within ten minutes.
4. Add the drippings of turkey in a pan, cream cheese and whipping cream. Simmer. Put pepper, soy sauce, and salt. Sauté the small capers in remaining butter.
5. Slice and serve with fried capers and cream cheese sauce.

Nutrition:

Calories: 810.3

Protein: 47.6g

Carbs: 6.9g

Fat: 68.6g

Fiber: 0.6g

48. Baked Salmon and Pesto

Preparation Time: 15 minutes

Cooking Time: 30 minutes

Servings: 4

Ingredients:

- For the green sauce:
- Four tablespoons. green pesto
- One cup mayonnaise
- Half cup Greek yogurt
- Pepper
- salt

For the salmon:

- Two pounds salmon
- Four tablespoons. green pesto
- Pepper
- salt

Directions:

1. Put the fillets on a greased baking dish with the skin side down. Add pesto on top. Add pepper and salt.
2. Bake at 200 degrees within thirty minutes.
3. Combine all the listed fixing for the green sauce in a bowl.
4. Serve the baked salmon with green sauce on top.

Nutrition:

Calories: 1010.2

Protein: 51.6g

Carbs: 3.1g

Fat: 87.6g

Fiber: 0.7g

49. Keto Chicken with Butter and Lemon

Preparation Time: 15 minutes

Cooking Time: 1 hour & 30 minutes

Servings: 2

Ingredients:

- Three pounds whole chicken
- Pepper and salt
- Two teaspoon barbecue seasoning
- Five ounces butter
- One lemon
- Two onions
- One-fourth cup water
- One teaspoon. butter

Directions:

1. Warm-up oven at 170 degrees. Grease the baking dish.
2. Rub the chicken with pepper, salt, and barbecue seasoning. Put in the baking dish.

3. Arrange lemon wedges and onions surrounding the chicken put slices of butter.
4. Bake within 1 hour and 30 minutes. Slice and serve.

Nutrition:

Calories: 980.3

Protein: 57.2g

Carbs: 0.4g

Fat: 81.3g

Fiber: 0.1g

50. Garlic Chicken

Preparation Time: 15 minutes

Cooking Time: 40 minutes

Servings: 4

Ingredients:

- Two ounces butter
- Two pounds chicken drumsticks
- Pepper
- salt
- lemon juice
- Two tablespoons. olive oil
- Seven cloves garlic
- Half cup parsley

Directions:

1. Warm-up oven at 250 degrees Celsius.
2. Put the chicken in a baking dish. Add pepper and salt.
3. Add olive oil with lemon juice over the chicken. Sprinkle parsley and garlic on top.
4. Bake within forty minutes. Serve.

Nutrition:

Calories: 540.3 Protein: 41.3g Carbs: 3.1g

Fat: 38.6g Fiber: 1.6g

51. Salmon Skewers Wrapped with Prosciutto

Preparation Time: 15 minutes

Cooking Time: 4 minutes

Servings: 4

Ingredients:

- 1/4cup basil
- One-pound salmon
- One pinch black pepper
- Four ounces prosciutto
- One tablespoon. olive oil
- Eight skewers

Directions:

1. Start by soaking the skewers in a bowl of water.
2. Cut the salmon fillets lengthwise. Thread the salmon using skewers.
3. Coat the skewers in pepper and basil. Wrap the slices of prosciutto around the salmon.
4. Warm-up oil in a grill pan. Grill the skewers within four minutes. Serve.

Nutrition:

Calories: 670.5

Protein: 27.2g

Carbs: 1.2g

Fat: 61.6g

Fiber: 0.3g

52. Buffalo Drumsticks and Chili Aioli

Preparation Time: 15 minutes

Cooking Time: 40 minutes

Servings: 4

Ingredients:

For the chili aioli:

- Half cup mayonnaise
- One tablespoon. smoked paprika powder
- One clove garlic

For the chicken:

- Two pounds chicken drumsticks
- Two tablespoons. of each:
- White wine vinegar
- Olive oil
- One tablespoon. tomato paste
- One teaspoon. each

- Salt
- Paprika powder
- Tabasco

Directions:

1. Warm up oven at 200 degrees.
2. Combine the listed marinade fixing. Marinate the chicken drumsticks within ten minutes.
3. Arrange the chicken drumsticks in the tray. Bake within forty minutes.
4. Combine the listed items for the chili aioli in a bowl. Serve.

Nutrition:

Calories: 567.8 Protein: 41.3g

Carbs: 2.2g Fat: 43.2g Fiber: 1.1g

53. Slow Cooked Roasted Pork and Creamy Gravy

Preparation Time: 15 minutes

Cooking Time: 8 hours & 15 minutes

Servings: 6

Ingredients:

For the creamy gravy:

- Two cups whipping cream

- Roast juice

For the pork:

- Two pounds pork roast
- Half tablespoon. salts
- One bay leaf
- Five black peppercorns
- Three cups of water
- Two teaspoon thyme
- Two cloves garlic
- Two ounces ginger
- One tablespoon. of each:
- Paprika powder
- Olive oil
- One-third teaspoon. black pepper

Directions:

1. Warm-up your oven at 100 degrees.

2. Add the meat, salt, water in a baking dish. Put peppercorns, thyme, and bay leaf. Put in the oven within eight hours. Remove. Reserve the juices. Adjust to 200 degrees.

3. Put ginger, garlic, pepper, herbs, and oil. Rub the herb mixture on the meat. Roast the pork within fifteen minutes.

4. Slice the roasted meat. Strain the meat juices in a bowl. Boil for reducing it by half.

5. Add the cream. Simmer within twenty minutes. Serve with creamy gravy.

Nutrition:

Calories: 586.9

Protein: 27.9g

Carbs: 2.6g

Fat: 50.3g

Fiber: 1.5g

54. Bacon-Wrapped Meatloaf

Preparation Time: 15 minutes

Cooking Time: 1 hour

Servings: 4

Ingredients:

For the meatloaf:

Two tablespoons. Butter

One onion

Two pounds beef

Half cup whipping cream

Two ounces cheese

One large egg

One tablespoon. oregano

One teaspoon. salt

Half teaspoon. black pepper

Seven ounces bacon

For the gravy:

1&1/2 cup whipping cream

Half tablespoon. tamari soy sauce

Directions:

Warm-up your oven at 200 degrees Celsius.

Dissolve the butter in a pan. Add the onion. Cook within four minutes. Keep aside.

Combine onion, ground meat, and the remaining fixing except for the bacon in a large bowl.

Make a firm loaf. Use bacon strips for wrapping the loaf.

Bake the meatloaf for forty-five minutes.

Put the juices from the baking dish and cream, then boil. Simmer within ten minutes. Add the soy sauce. Slice and serve with gravy.

Nutrition:

Calories: 1020.3

Protein: 46.7g

Carbs: 5.6g

Fat: 88.9g

Fiber: 1.2g

55. Lamb Chops and Herb Butter

Preparation Time: 15 minutes

Cooking Time: 4 minutes

Servings: 4

Ingredients:

- Eight lamb chops
- One tablespoon. each:
- Olive oil
- Butter
- Pepper
- salt
- For the herb butter:
- Five ounces butter
- One clove garlic
- Half tablespoon. garlic powder
- Four tablespoons. parsley
- One teaspoon. lemon juice
- One-third teaspoon. salt

Directions:

1. Season the lamb chops with pepper and salt.

2. Warm-up olive oil and butter in an iron skillet. Add the lamb chops. Fry within four minutes.

3. Mix all the listed items for the herb butter in a bowl. Cool.

4. Serve with herb butter.

Nutrition:

Calories: 722.3

Protein: 42.3g

Carbs: 0.4g

Fat: 61.5g

Fiber: 0.4g

56. Crispy Cuban Pork Roast

Preparation Time: 15 minutes

Cooking Time: 4 minutes

Servings: 6

Ingredients:

- Five pounds pork shoulder
- Four teaspoon salt
- Two teaspoon. cumin
- One teaspoon. black pepper
- Two tablespoons. oregano
- One red onion
- Four cloves garlic

- orange juice
- lemons juiced
- One-fourth cup of olive oil

Directions:

1. Rub the pork shoulder with salt in a bowl. Mix all the remaining items of the marinade in a blender.

2. Marinate the meat within eight hours. Cook within forty minutes. Warm-up your oven at 200 degrees. Roast the pork within thirty minutes.

3. Remove the meat juice. Simmer within twenty minutes. Shred the meat.

4. Pour the meat juice. Serve.

Nutrition:

Calories: 910.3

Protein: 58.3g

Carbs: 5.3g

Fat: 69.6g

Fiber: 2.2g

57. Keto Barbecued Ribs

Preparation Time: 15 minutes

Cooking Time: 1 hour & 10 minutes

Servings: 4

Ingredients:

- One-fourth cup Dijon mustard
- Two tablespoons. of each:
- Cider vinegar

- Butter
- Salt
- Three pounds of spare ribs
- Four tablespoons. paprika powder
- Half tablespoon. chili powder
- 1&1/2 tablespoon. garlic powder
- Two teaspoon. of each:
- Onion powder
- Cumin
- Two & 1/2 tablespoon. black pepper

Directions:

1. Warm-up a grill for thirty minutes.
2. Mix vinegar and Dijon mustard in a bowl, put the ribs and coat.
3. Mix all the listed spices. Rub the mix all over the ribs. Put aside. Put ribs on an aluminum foil. Add some butter over the ribs. Wrap with foil. Grill within one hour. Remove and slice.
4. Put the reserved spice mix. Grill again within ten minutes. Serve.

Nutrition:

Calories: 980.3

Protein: 54.3g

Carbs: 5.8g

Fat: 80.2g

Fiber: 4.6g

58. Turkey Burgers and Tomato Butter

Preparation Time: 15 minutes

Cooking Time: 15 minutes

Servings: 4

Ingredients:

For the chicken patties:

- Two pounds of chicken
- One egg
- Half onion
- One teaspoon. salt
- Half teaspoon. black pepper
- One a half teaspoon. thyme
- Two ounces butter
- For the fried cabbage:
- Two pounds green cabbage
- Three ounces butter
- One teaspoon. salt
- Half teaspoon. black pepper (ground)
- For the tomato butter:
- Four ounces butter
- One tablespoon. tomato paste
- One teaspoon. red wine vinegar
- Pepper
- salt

Directions:

1. Warm-up your oven at 100 degrees.
2. Combine the listed items for the patties in a large bowl. Shape the mixture into patties.
3. Fry the chicken patties for five minutes, each side. Keep warm in the oven.
4. Warm-up butter in a pan. Put the cabbage, plus pepper and salt. Fry for five minutes.
5. Whip the items for the tomato butter in a bowl using an electric mixer.
6. Serve with a dollop of tomato butter from the top.

Nutrition:

Calories: 830.4

Protein: 33.6g

Carbs: 6.7g

Fat: 71.5g

Fiber: 5.1g

59. Keto Hamburger

Preparation Time: 15 minutes

Cooking Time: 70 minutes

Servings: 4

Ingredients:

For the burger buns:

- Two cups almond flour
- Five tablespoons. ground psyllium husk powder
- Two teaspoon. baking powder
- One teaspoon. salt
- 1&1/2 cup water
- Two teaspoon. cider vinegar
- Three egg whites
- One tablespoon. sesame seed
- For the hamburger:
- Two pounds beef
- 1-ounce olive oil
- Pepper and salt
- 1&1/2-ounce lettuce
- One tomato
- One red onion
- Half cup mayonnaise
- Five ounces bacon

Directions:

1. Warm-up your oven at 150 degrees.
2. Mix the listed dry items for the buns in a bowl. Boil the water. Put egg whites, water, and vinegar to the dry mix. Mix.
3. Make individual pieces of buns, put sesame seeds on the top. Bake for sixty minutes
4. Fry the slices of bacon. Keep aside.
5. Mix beef, pepper, and salt in a bowl. Make patties. Grill the beef patties for five minutes, each side.

6. Combine mayonnaise and lettuce in a bowl. Cut the buns in half. Add beef patty, lettuce mix, onion slice, and a tomato slice. Top with bacon slices. Serve.

Nutrition:

Calories: 1070.3

Protein: 53.4g

Carbs: 6.1g

Fat: 85.3g

Fiber: 12.3g

60. Keto Buffalo Chicken Empanadas

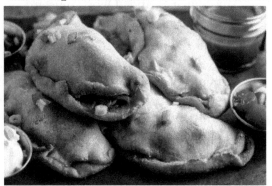

Preparation Time: 20 minutes

Cooking Time: 30 minutes

Servings: 6

Ingredients:

For the empanada dough

- 1 ½ cups mozzarella cheese
- 3 oz cream cheese
- 1 whisked egg
- 2 cups almond flour

For the buffalo chicken filling

- 2 cups shredded chicken
- 2 tablespoons Butter
- 0.33 cup Hot Sauce

Directions:

1. Warm-up oven, 425-degrees.

2. Microwave the cheese & cream cheese within 1-minute. Stir the flour and egg into the dish.

3. With another bowl, combine the chicken with sauce and set aside.

4. Cover a flat surface with plastic wrap and sprinkle with almond flour.

5. Grease a rolling pin, press the dough flat.

6. Make the circle shapes out of this dough with a lid.

7. Portion out spoonful of filling into these dough circles.

8. Fold the other half over to close up into half-moon shapes.

9. Bake within 9 minutes. Serve.

Nutrition:

Net carbs: 20g Fiber: 0g Fat: 96g Protein: 74g

Calories: 1217kcal

61. Pepperoni and Cheddar Stromboli

Preparation Time: 15 minutes

Cooking Time: 20 minutes

Servings: 3

Ingredients:

- -1.25 cups Mozzarella Cheese

- 0.25 cup Almond Flour

- 3 tablespoons Coconut Flour

- 1 teaspoon Italian Seasoning

- 1 Egg

- 6 oz Deli Ham

- 2 oz Pepperoni

- 4 oz Cheddar Cheese

- 1 tablespoon Butter

- 6 cups Salad Greens

Directions:

1. Warm-up the oven, 400 degrees.

2. Melt the mozzarella. Mix flours & Italian seasoning in a separate bowl.

3. Dump in the melty cheese and mix with pepper and salt.

4. Stir in the egg and process the dough. Pour it onto that prepared baking tray.

5. Roll out the dough. Cut slits that mark out 4 equal rectangles.

6. Put the ham and cheese, then brush with butter and close up.

7. Bake within 17 minutes. Slice and serve.

Nutrition:

Net carbs: 20g Fiber: 0g Fat: 13g Protein: 11g

Calories: 240kcal

62. Tuna Casserole

Preparation Time: 15 minutes

Cooking Time: 10 minutes

Servings: 4

Ingredients:

- Tuna in oil, sixteen ounces

- Butter two tablespoons

- Salt

- Black pepper

- Chili powder, one teaspoon

- Celery, six stalks
- Green bell pepper, one
- Yellow onion, one
- Parmesan cheese, grated four ounces
- Mayonnaise, one cup

Directions:

1. Warm-up oven to 400.
2. Fry the onion, bell pepper, and celery chops in the melted butter within five minutes.
3. Mix with the chili powder, parmesan cheese, tuna, and mayonnaise.
4. Grease a baking pan. Add the tuna mixture into the fried vegetables.
5. Bake within twenty minutes. Serve.

Nutrition:

Calories 953 5g net carbs 83g fat 43g protein

63. Brussels Sprout and Hamburger Gratin

Preparation Time: 15 minutes

Cooking Time: 20 minutes

Servings: 4

Ingredients:

- Ground beef, one pound

- Bacon, eight ounces
- Brussel sprouts, fifteen ounces
- Salt
- Black pepper
- Thyme; one half teaspoon
- Cheddar cheese, one cup
- Italian seasoning; one tablespoon
- Sour cream; four tablespoons
- Butter; two tablespoons

Directions:

1. Warm-up oven to 425.
2. Fry bacon and Brussel sprouts in butter within five minutes.
3. Stir in the sour cream and put into a greased baking pan.
4. Cook the ground beef and put salt and pepper, then add this mix to the baking pan.
5. Top with the herbs and the shredded cheese. Bake within twenty minutes. Serve.

Nutrition:

Calories: 770kcal Net carbs: 8g Fat: 62g

Protein: 42g

64. Carpaccio

Preparation Time: 15 minutes

Cooking Time: 5 minutes

Servings: 4

Ingredients:

- 100 grams smoked prime rib
- 30 grams arugula
- 20 grams Parmesan cheese
- 10 grams pine nuts
- 7 grams of butter
- 3 tablespoons olive oil with orange

- 1 tablespoon lemon juice
- Pepper
- salt

Directions:

1. Arrange the meat slices on a plate. Place the arugula on top of the meat.
2. Spread Parmesan cheese over the arugula.
3. Put the butter in a frying pan. Add the pine nuts, bake for a few minutes over medium heat and then sprinkle them over the carpaccio.
4. For the vinaigrette, mix the lemon juice into the olive oil, put pepper and salt and drizzle over the carpaccio. Serve.

Nutrition:

Calories: 350 kcal Protein: 31 g

Fat: 24 g Fiber: 1 g

carbohydrates: 2 g

65. Keto Croque Monsieur

Preparation Time: 15 minutes

Cooking Time: 7 minutes

Servings: 4

Ingredients:

- 2 eggs
- 25 grams grated cheese

- 25 grams ham
- 40 ml of cream
- 40 ml mascarpone
- 30 grams of butter
- Pepper
- salt
- Basil leaves

Directions:

1. Beat eggs in a bowl, put salt and pepper.
2. Add the cream, mascarpone, and grated cheese and mix.
3. Melt the butter over medium heat. Adjust the heat to low.
4. Add half of the omelet mixture to the frying pan and then place the slice of ham. Put the rest of the omelet mixture over the ham. Fry within 2-3 minutes over low heat.
5. Then put the omelet back in the frying pan to fry for another 1-2 minutes.
6. Garnish with a few basil leaves. Serve.

Nutrition:

Calories: 350 kcal Protein: 31 g Fat: 24 g

Fiber: 1 g carbohydrates: 2 g

66. Keto Wraps with Cream Cheese and Salmon

Preparation Time: 15 minutes

Cooking Time: 10 minutes

Servings: 4

Ingredients:

- 80 grams of cream cheese
- 1 tablespoon dill
- 30 grams smoked salmon
- 1 egg
- 15 grams of butter
- Pinch cayenne pepper

- Pepper
- salt

Directions:

1. Beat the egg well in a bowl.
2. Dissolve the butter over medium heat in a small frying pan. Put half of the beaten egg to the pan.
3. Carefully loosen the egg on the edges with a silicone spatula and turn the wafer-thin omelet, about 45 seconds each side. Remove.
4. Cut the dill into small pieces and put them in a bowl.
5. Add the cream cheese and the salmon, cut into small pieces. Mix.
6. Put a cayenne pepper and mix. Put salt and pepper.
7. Spread a layer on the wrap and roll it up. Cut the wrap in half and serve.

Nutrition:

Calories: 479 kcal Protein: 16 g Fats: 45 g

Net carbohydrates: 4 g

67. Savory Keto Broccoli Cheese Muffins

Preparation Time: 15 minutes

Cooking Time: 10 minutes

Servings: 4

Ingredients:

- 4 eggs
- 75 grams Parmesan cheese
- 125 grams young cheese
- 125 grams mozzarella
- 75 grams of broccoli
- -1.5 teaspoon baking powder
- 0.25 teaspoon garlic powder
- 0.25 teaspoon mustard

Directions:

1. Warm-up oven to 160° Celsius.
2. Boil water into a saucepan, put the broccoli pieces, for 1 minute. Drain.
3. Grate the Parmesan cheese and the young cheese. Cut the mozzarella into small pieces.
4. Beat the eggs, put the broccoli, cheese, and mustard.
5. Then add the garlic powder and baking powder and mix.
6. Add baking powder and garlic powder.
7. Fill a silicone muffin tray with the broccoli-cheese egg batter and bake within 10 minutes. Serve.

Nutrition:

Calories: 349 kcal

Protein: 28 g

Fats: 25 g

Fiber: 1 g

Carbohydrates: 3 g

68. Keto Rusk

Preparation Time: 15 minutes
Cooking Time: 9 minutes
Servings: 6
Ingredients:

- 35 grams of almond flour
- 1 egg
- 1 tablespoon butter
- 0.5 teaspoon baking powder
- 1/8 teaspoon salt

Directions:

1. Warm-up oven to 200° Celsius. Put all the fixing in a cup and mix.
2. Microwave within 90 seconds.
3. Cool down and cut the dough into 5 equal slices and place it on a sheet with baking paper.
4. Bake for 5-6 minutes then serve.

Nutrition:
Calories: 53 kcal
Protein: 2 g
Fats: 4 g
Carbohydrates: 1 g

69. Flaxseed Hemp Flour Bun

Preparation Time: 15 minutes
Cooking Time: 8 minutes
Servings: 4
Ingredients:

- 1 teaspoon hemp flour
- 1 teaspoon linseed flour
- 1 teaspoon psyllium
- 1 teaspoon baking powder
- 1 egg
- 0.5 teaspoon butter

Directions:

1. Warm-up oven to 180°C. Put all dry items in a large cup, mix.
2. Add the egg and the butter then mix it again. Microwave within 1 minute.
3. Remove the sandwich and cut it into three slices. Bake those slices within 5 minutes. Serve.

Nutrition:
Calories: 182 kcal Protein: 11g Fats: 15g
Fiber: 12 g

70. Keto Muffins with Roquefort

Preparation Time: 15 minutes
Cooking Time: 18 minutes
Servings: 4
Ingredients:

- 150 grams zucchini
- 50 ml extra virgin olive oil
- Pepper
- 100 grams red pepper
- 75 grams Roquefort
- 100 grams mascarpone
- 6 eggs
- -1.5 teaspoon baking powder

Directions:

1. Warm-up oven to 175° Celsius.
2. Fry the zucchini and bell pepper within 5 minutes. Beat the eggs with the baking powder.
3. Mix the vegetables, the butter, mascarpone, and cheese and put over the muffin tins.
4. Bake within 15 minutes. Serve.

Nutrition:
Calories: 160 kcal Protein: 6g Fats: 14g
Fiber: 1g Carbohydrates: 1g

CHAPTER 6:

Snacks and Cakes

71. Keto Raspberry Cake and White Chocolate Sauce

Preparation Time: 15 minutes

Cooking Time: 45 minutes

Servings: 4

Ingredients:

- 5 ounces cacao butter
- 4 teaspoons pure vanilla extract
- 4 eggs
- 3 cup raspberries
- 2½ ounces grass-fed ghee
- 1 teaspoon baking powder
- 1 tablespoon apple cider vinegar
- 1 cup green banana flour
- ¾ cup coconut cream
- ¾ cup granulated sweetener
- 4 ounces cacao butter
- 2 teaspoons pure vanilla extract
- ¾ cup coconut cream
- salt

Directions:

1. Mix the butter and the sweetener. Pour in the grass-fed ghee into the mix, blend.
2. Beat the eggs in a different bowl.
3. Warm-up oven to 350 degrees F. Grease a baking pan.
4. Put the mixed eggs to the butter and sweetener mixture. Mix well.
5. Pour in the banana flour and mix. Then the vanilla extract, apple cider, coconut cream, baking powder, and mix again.
6. Spoon around the sliced raspberries. Then, sprinkle flour in the baking pan.
7. Put the mixture into the pan then bake within 45 minutes. Cool down.
8. For the sauce
9. Mix cacao butter with 2 teaspoons pure vanilla extract. Add coconut cream and beat. Put salt and beat. Chop the remaining berries and throw them in the mix. Pour the mix on the cake. Serve cold.

Nutrition:

Calories: 325 kcal

Total Fat: 12g

Total Carbs: 3g

Protein: 40g

72. Keto Chocolate Chip Cookies

Preparation Time: 15 minutes

Cooking Time: 10 minutes

Servings: 4

Ingredients:

- 7 spoons unsweetened coconut powder
- 7 tablespoons Keto chocolate chips
- 5 tablespoons butter
- 2 flat tablespoon baking powder
- 2 eggs
- 2/3 confectioners swerve
- 1 1/3 cups almond flour
- A teaspoon vanilla extract

Directions

1. Warm-up oven to 325.
2. Melt half chocolate chips, then the butter. Mix.
3. Mix the eggs in chocolate and butter mixture.
4. Mix in the vanilla extract, coconut powder, confectioners swerve, and almond flour. Mix well.
5. Add chocolate chip cookies. Then, add baking powder, and mix until dough forms.

6. Spread out and cut out cookies, top with chocolate chips.
7. Bake within 8 to 10 minutes. Serve.

Nutrition:

Calories: 287 kcal

Total Fat: 19g

Total Carbs: 6.5g

Protein: 6.8g

73. Keto Beef and Sausage Balls

Preparation Time: 15 minutes

Cooking Time: 20 minutes

Servings: 3

Ingredients:

- Meat
- 2 pounds ground beef
- 2 pounds ground sausage
- 2 eggs
- ½ cup Keto mayonnaise
- 1/3 cup ground pork rinds
- ½ cup Parmesan cheese
- Salt
- Pepper
- 2 tablespoons butter
- 3 tablespoons oil

Sauce

- 3 diced onions
- 2 pounds mushrooms
- 5 cloves garlic

- 3 cups beef broth
- 1 cup sour cream
- 2 tablespoons mustard
- Worcestershire sauce
- Salt
- Pepper
- Parsley
- 1 tablespoon Arrowroot powder

Directions:

1. Put meat, egg, and onions in a bowl, mix. Put beef, parmesan, egg, mayonnaise, sausage, pork rind in a bowl. Add salt and pepper. Warm-up oil in a skillet.

2. Mold the beef mixture into balls, fry within 7-10 minutes. Put aside.

3. Fry the diced onions, then the garlic and mushrooms, cook within 3 minutes. Then, add the broth.

4. Mix in mustard, sour cream, and Worcestershire sauce. Boil within two minutes, then adds in the meatballs. Add salt and pepper, simmer. Serve.

Nutrition:

Calories: 592 kcal

Total Fat: 53.9g

Total Carbs: 1.3g

Protein: 25.4g

74. Keto Coconut Flake Balls

Preparation Time: 15 minutes

Cooking Time: 0 minutes

Servings: 2

Ingredients:

- 1 Vanilla Shortbread Collagen Protein Bar
- 1 tablespoon lemon
- ¼ teaspoon ground ginger

- ½ cup unsweetened coconut flakes,
- ¼ teaspoon ground turmeric

Directions:

1. Process protein bar, ginger, turmeric, and ¾ of the total bits into a food processor.

2. Remove and add a spoon of water and roll till dough forms.

3. Roll into balls, and sprinkle the rest of the flakes on it. Serve.

Nutrition:

Calories: 204 kcal

Total Fat: 11g

Total Carbs: 4.2g

Protein: 1.5g

75. Keto Chocolate Greek Yoghurt Cookies

Preparation Time: 15 minutes

Cooking Time: 30 minutes

Servings: 3

Ingredients:

- 3 eggs
- 1/8 teaspoon tartar
- 5 tablespoons softened Greek yogurt

Directions:

1. Beat the egg whites, the tartar, and mix.

2. In the yolk, put in the Greek yogurt, and mix.

3. Combine both egg whites and yolk batter into a bowl.

4. Bake within 25-30 minutes, serve.

Nutrition:

Calories: 287 kcal

Total Fat: 19g

Total Carbs: 6.5g

Protein: 6.8g

76. Keto coconut flavored ice cream

Preparation Time: 15 minutes

Cooking Time: 0 minutes

Servings: 4

Ingredients:

4 cups of coconut milk

2/3 cup xylitol

¼ teaspoon salt

2 teaspoons vanilla extract

1 teaspoon coconut extract

Directions:

Add the coconut milk in a bowl, with the sweetener, extracts, and salt. Mix.

Pour this mixture in the ice cube trays, and put it in the freezer. Serve.

Nutrition:

Calories: 244 kcal

Total Fat: 48g

Total Carbs: 6g

Protein: 15g

77. Chocolate-Coconut Cookies

Preparation Time: 15 minutes

Cooking Time: 20 minutes

Servings: 4

Ingredients:

- 2 eggs
- ½ cup of cocoa powder
- ½ cup flour
- ½ cup of coconut oil
- ¼ cup grated coconut
- Stevia

Directions:

1. Warm-up oven to 350 °F. Crack eggs and separate whites and yolks, mix separately.

2. Put salt to the yolks. Warm-up oil in a skillet, and add cocoa, egg whites, mixing, add in the salted yolks. Then, add stevia. Add in coconut flour, and mix until dough forms.

3. On a flat surface, sprinkle grated coconut. Roll the dough around in the coconut, mix. Mold into cookies. Bake within 15 minutes, serve.

Nutrition:

Calories: 260 kcal

Total Fat: 26g

Total Carbs: 4.5g

Protein: 1g

78. Keto Buffalo Chicken Meatballs

Preparation Time: 15 minutes

Cooking Time: 20 minutes

Servings: 3

Ingredients:

- 1-pound ground chicken
- 1 large
- 2/3 cup hot sauce
- ½ cup almond flour
- ½ teaspoon salt

- ½ teaspoon pepper
- ½ cup melted butter
- 1 large onion
- 1 teaspoon garlic

Directions:

1. Combine meat, egg, and onions in a bowl. Pour in almond flour, garlic, salt, and pepper in.
2. Warm-up oven to 350°F and grease a baking tray.
3. Mold the egg mixture into balls. Bake within 18-20 minutes.
4. Melt butter in the microwave for few seconds; mix it with hot sauce.
5. Put the sauce into meatballs. Serve.

Nutrition:

Calories: 360 kcal

Total Fat: 26g

Total Carbs: 4.5g

Protein: 1g

79. Eggplant And Chickpea Bites

Preparation Time: 15 minutes

Cooking Time: 90 minutes

Servings: 6

Ingredients:

- 3 large aubergines
- Spray oil
- 2 large cloves garlic
- 2 tablespoon. coriander powder
- 2 tablespoon. cumin seeds
- 400 g canned chickpeas
- 2 Tablespoon. chickpea flour
- Zest and juice 1/2 lemon
- 1/2 lemon quartered
- 3 tablespoon. tablespoon polenta

Directions:

1. Warm-up oven to 200°C. Grease the eggplant halves and place it on the meat side up on a baking sheet.
2. Sprinkle with coriander and cumin seeds, and then place the cloves of garlic on the plate. Roast within 40 minutes, put aside.
3. Add chickpeas, chickpea flour, zest, and lemon juice. Crush roughly and mix well.
4. Form about twenty pellets and place them on a baking sheet. Fridge within 30 minutes.
5. Warm-up oven to 180°C. Remove the meatballs from the fridge and coat it in the polenta. Roast for 20 minutes. Serve with lemon wedges.

Nutrition:

Calories: 70

Carbs: 4g

Fat: 5g

Protein: 2g

80. Baba Ganoush

Preparation Time: 15 minutes

Cooking Time: 20 minutes

Servings: 3

Ingredients:

- 1 large aubergine
- 1 head of garlic
- 30 ml of olive oil
- Lemon juice

Directions:

1. Warm-up oven to 350 ° F.
2. Place the eggplant on the plate, skin side up. Roast, about 1 hour.
3. Place the garlic cloves in a square of aluminum foil. Fold the edges of the sheet. Roast with the eggplant, about 20 minutes. Let cool. Purée the pods with a garlic press.
4. Puree the flesh of the eggplant. Add the garlic puree, the oil, and the lemon juice.
5. Serve.

Nutrition:

Calories: 87

Carbs: 6g

Fat: 6g

Protein: 2g

81. Spicy Crab Dip

Preparation Time: 15 minutes

Cooking Time: 20 minutes

Servings: 3

Ingredients:

- 8 oz cream cheese
- 1 tablespoon. onions
- 1 tablespoon. lemon juice
- 2 tablespoon. Worcestershire sauce
- 1/8 teaspoon. t. black
- Cayenne pepper
- 2 tablespoon. milk
- 6 oz crabmeat

Directions:

1. Warm-up oven to 375 ° F.
2. Pour the cream cheese into a bowl. Add the onions, lemon juice, Worcestershire sauce, black pepper, and cayenne pepper. Mix. Stir in the milk and crab meat.
3. Cook uncovered within 15 minutes. Serve.

Nutrition:

Calories: 134 Carbs: 4g

Fat: 12g Protein: 4g

82. Potatoes" of Parmesan cheese

Preparation Time: 15 minutes

Cooking Time: 10 minutes

Servings: 3

Ingredients:

- 75 g Parmesan cheese
- 1 tablespoon Chia seeds
- 2 tablespoon whole flaxseeds
- 2½ tablespoon pumpkin seeds

Directions:

1. Warm-up oven to 180 ° C.
2. Combine both the cheese and seeds in a bowl.
3. Put small piles of the mixture on the baking paper, bake within 8 to 10 minutes
4. Remove and serve.

Nutrition:

Calories: 165

Carbs: 18g

Fat: 9g

Protein: 3g

83. Chili Cheese Chicken with Crispy and Delicious Cabbage Salad

Preparation Time: 15 minutes

Cooking Time: 70 minutes

Servings: 5

Ingredients:

- Chili Cheese Chicken
- 400 grams of chicken
- 200 grams tomatoes
- 100 grams of cream cheese
- 125 grams cheddar
- 40 grams jalapenos
- 60 grams of bacon
- Crispy Cabbage Salad
- 0.5 pcs casserole
- 200 grams Brussels sprouts
- 2 grams of almonds
- 3 paragraph mandarins
- 1 tablespoon olive oil
- 1 teaspoon apple cider vinegar
- 0.5 teaspoon salt
- 0.25 teaspoon pepper
- 1 tablespoon lemon

Directions:

1. Warm-up oven at 200 °. Put tomatoes half in the bottom of a baking dish. Put chicken fillets, half cream cheese on each chicken fillet, and sprinkle with cheddar.
2. Spread jalapenos and bake within 25 minutes. Place bacon on a baking sheet with baking paper, and bake within 10 minutes.
3. For cabbage salad:
4. Blend the Brussels sprouts and cumin in a food processor.
5. Make the dressing of juice from one mandarin, olive oil, apple cider vinegar, salt, pepper, and lemon juice.
6. Put the cabbage in a dish and spread the dressing over. Chop almonds, cut the tangerine into slices and place it on the salad. Sprinkle the bacon over the chicken dish. Serve.

Nutrition:

Calories: 515

Carbs: 35g

Fat: 23g

Protein: 42g

84. Keto Pumpkin Pie Sweet and Spicy

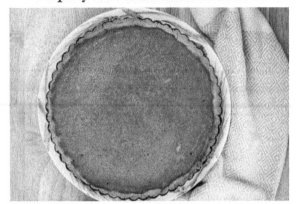

Preparation Time: 15 minutes

Cooking Time: 60 minutes

Servings: 5

Ingredients:

Pie Bottom

- 110 grams of almond flour
- 50 grams serine
- 0.5 teaspoon salt
- 1 scoop protein powder
- 1 paragraph eggs
- 80 grams of butter
- 15 grams of fiber

The Filling

- 1 pcs Hokkaido
- 3 paragraph egg yolks
- 60 ml of coconut fat
- 1 teaspoon vanilla powder
- 15 grams of protein powder
- 1 teaspoon cinnamon
- 2 grams sucrine
- 0.5 teaspoon cardamom Bla
- 0.5 teaspoon cloves

Directions:

1. Warm-up oven to 175 °.

2. Combine all the dry fixing and add the wet ones. Mix and shape it into a dough lump. Put in a baking paper, then flatten the dough. Prick holes then bake within 8-10 minutes.

3. For filling:

4. Cut the meat of Hokkaido and cook within 15-20 minutes. Process it with the other fixing. Pour the stuffing into the baked pie and bake again within 25-30 minutes. Cool and serve.

Nutrition:

Calories: 229

Carbs: 4g

Fat: 22g

Protein: 8g

85. Blackened Tilapia with Zucchini Noodles

Preparation Time: 15 minutes

Cooking Time: 10 minutes

Servings: 5

Ingredients:

2 zucchinis

¾ teaspoon salt

2 garlic cloves

1 cup Pico de Gallo

1 ½ pounds fish

2 teaspoons olive oil

½ teaspoon cumin

¼ teaspoon garlic powder

½ paprika

½ teaspoon pepper

Directions:

Mix half salt, pepper, cumin, paprika, and garlic powder, rub to the fish thoroughly. Cook within 3 minutes each side and remove it. Cook zucchini and garlic, remaining salt within 2 minutes. Serve.

Nutrition:

Calories: 220

Carbs: 27g

Fat: 2g

Protein: 24g

86. Bell Pepper Nachos

Preparation Time: 15 minutes

Cooking Time: 10 minutes

Servings: 2

Ingredients:

- 2 bell peppers
- 4 ounces beef ground
- ¼ teaspoon cumin
- ¼ cup guacamole
- salt

- 1 cup cheese
- ¼ teaspoon chili powder
- 1 tablespoon vegetable oil
- 2 tablespoons sour cream
- ¼ cup Pico de Gallo

Directions:

1. Put the bell peppers in a microwave dish, sprinkle salt and splash water on it and microwave within 4 minutes and cut it in 4 pieces.
2. Toast the chili powder and cumin in the pan for 30 seconds. Put the salted beef, stir and cook within 4 minutes.
3. Put on all the pieces of pepper. Add cheese and cook within 1 minute. Serve with Pico de Gallo, guacamole, and cream.

Nutrition:

Calories: 475 Carbs: 19g Fat: 24g Protein: 50g

87. Radish, Carrot & Cilantro Salad

Preparation Time: 15 minutes

Cooking Time: 0 minutes

Servings: 2

Ingredients:

- 1 ½ pounds carrots
- ¼ cup cilantro

- 1 ½ pound radish
- ½ teaspoon salt
- 6 onions
- ¼ teaspoon black pepper
- 3 tablespoons lemon juice
- 3 tablespoons orange juice
- 2 tablespoons olive oil

Directions:

1. Mix all the items until they merged adequately. Chill and serve.

Nutrition:

Calories: 33 Carbs: 7g

Fat: 0g Protein: 0g

88. Asparagus-Mushroom Frittata

Preparation Time: 15 minutes

Cooking Time: 25 minutes

Servings: 2

Ingredients:

- 1 tablespoon olive oil
- 1garlic clove
- ¼ cup onion
- 2 cups button mushrooms

- 1 asparagus
- 1 tablespoon thyme
- 6 eggs
- ½ cup feta cheese
- salt
- black pepper

Directions:

1. Cook onions within 5 minutes. Put mushroom plus garlic then cook within 5 minutes. Mix thyme, salt, pepper, and asparagus and cook within 3 minutes.

2. Beat eggs and cheese in a bowl and pour it in the pan and cook for 2 to 3 minutes. Bake within 10 minutes.

Nutrition

Calories: 129 Carbs: 2g Fat: 7g Protein: 9g

89. Shrimp Avocado Salad

Preparation Time: 15 minutes

Cooking Time: 0 minutes

Servings: 1

Ingredients:

- 1/4cup onion
- 1 tomato

- 2 limes juice
- 1 avocado
- 1/4 teaspoon salt
- black pepper
- 1 jalapeno
- 1lb shrimp
- 1tablespoon cilantro

Directions:

1. Mix onion, lime juice, salt and pepper leave within 5 minutes. In another bowl, add chopped shrimp, avocado, tomato, jalapeno and onion mixture. Put salt and pepper, toss and serve.

Nutrition:

Calories: 365

Carbs: 15g

Fat: 17g

Protein: 25g

90. Smoky Cauliflower Bites

Preparation Time: 15 minutes

Cooking Time: 25 minutes

Servings: 2

Ingredients:

- 1 cauliflower
- 2 garlic cloves

- 2tablespoon olive oil
- 2tablespoon parsley
- 1teaspoon paprika
- 3/4teaspoon salt

Directions:

1. Mix cauliflower, olive oil, paprika and salt. Warm-up oven at 450. Bake within 10 minutes. Put garlic and bake within 10 to 15 minutes. Serve with parsley.

Nutrition:

Calories: 69

Carbs: 8g

Fat: 3g

Protein: 1g

91. Avocado Crab Boats

Preparation Time: 15 minutes

Cooking Time: 2 minutes

Servings: 2

Ingredients:

- 12oz lump crab meat
- 3tablespoon lemon juice
- 1/3cup Greek yogurt
- 1/2teaspoon pepper

- 1/2 onion
- Salt
- 2tablespoon chives
- 1cup cheddar cheese
- 2 avocados

Directions:

1. Mix meat, yogurt, onion, chives, lemon juice, cayenne and salt. Scoop the avocado flesh, fill the avocado bowl with meat mixture and top with cheddar cheese.
2. Microwave within 2 minutes and serve.

Nutrition:

Calories: 325 Carbs: 8g

Fat: 28g

Protein: 0g

92. Coconut Curry Cauliflower Soup

Preparation Time: 15 minutes

Cooking Time: 40 minutes

Servings: 2

Ingredients:

- 1tablespoon olive oil
- 2-3 teaspoon curry powder
- 1 onion
- 2teaspoon ground cumin
- 3 garlic cloves
- 1/2teaspoon turmeric powder
- 1teaspoon ginger
- 14oz coconut milk
- 14oz tomatoes
- 1cup vegetable broth
- 1 cauliflower
- Salt
- pepper

Directions:

1. Mix olive oil and onion in a pot, sauté within 3 minutes. Put garlic, ginger, curry powder, cumin and turmeric powder and sauté within 5 minutes.
2. Put coconut milk, tomatoes, vegetable broth and cauliflower. Cook on low within 20 minutes, blend the mixture through blender and warm-up the soup within 5 minutes. Put salt and pepper. Serve.

Nutrition:

Calories: 112

Carbs: 0g

Fat: 0g

Protein: 0g

93. Parmesan Asparagus

Preparation Time: 15 minutes

Cooking Time: 15 minutes

Servings: 4

Ingredients:

- 4lb asparagus
- Salt
- 1/4lb butter
- 2cups parmesan cheese shredded
- 1/2teaspoon pepper

Directions:

1. Boil asparagus within 3 minutes. Drain and put aside. Preheat oven at 350.
2. Arrange asparagus into the pan and pour butter, sprinkle pepper, salt and parmesan cheese. Bake within 10 to 15 minutes. Serve.

Nutrition:

Calories: 83

Carbs: 5g

Fat: 5g

Protein: 6g

94. Cream Cheese Pancakes

Preparation Time: 15 minutes

Cooking Time: 10 minutes

Servings: 12

Ingredients:

- 4oz cream cheese
- Vanilla extract
- 4eggs
- Butter

Directions:

1. Blend cream cheese and eggs in a blender, put aside. Grease skillet with butter. Cook the batter within 2 minutes. Serve with sprinkle cinnamon.

Nutrition:

Calories: 344

Carbs: 3g

Fat: 29g

Protein: 17g

95. Sugar-Free Mexican Spiced Dark Chocolate

Preparation Time: 15 minutes

Cooking Time: 0 minutes

Servings: 1

Ingredients:

- 1/2cup cocoa powder
- 1/4teaspoon cinnamon
- 1/2teaspoon chili powder
- 1/8teaspoon nutmeg
- black pepper
- salt
- 1/4cup melted butter
- 1/4teaspoon vanilla extract
- 25 drops liquid stevia

Directions:

1. Mix cocoa powder, cinnamon, chili powder, nutmeg, black pepper and salt. Put aside.

2. Stir melted butter with vanilla extract and stevia and mix butter mixture with dry items. Put the mixture in chocolate molds. Chill and serve.

Nutrition:

Calories: 60

Carbs: 8g

Fat: 5g

Protein: 1g

96. Tuna in Cucumber Cups

Preparation time: 15 minutes

Cooking time: 0 minutes

Servings: 10

Ingredients:

- Mayonnaise, 1/3cup
- Dill
- Black pepper, 1teaspoon
- Tuna, 1can
- Cucumber, 1

Directions:

1. Mix the cucumber flesh with the remainder of the fixing and then fill the holes in the slices of cucumber. Garnish with fresh dill. Serve.

Nutrition:

Calories 22

3 grams of protein

2 grams of fat

2 grams carbs

97. Parmesan Crisps

Preparation time: 15 minutes

Cooking time: 10 minutes

Servings: 2

Ingredients:

- Provolone cheese, 2

- Jalapeno pepper
- Parmesan cheese

Directions:

1. Warm-up oven to 425. Grease a baking sheet then set the eight tablespoons of parmesan cheese. Lay the slices of jalapeno over the parmesan cheese mounds.

2. Put one square provolone over the eight parmesan mounds. Bake within nine minutes and serve.

Nutrition:

Calories 160 15g protein 9g fat 2g carbs

98. Onion Rings

Preparation time: 15 minutes

Cooking time: 15 minutes

Servings: 2

Ingredients:

- 2 Eggs
- 1/2c Parmesan cheese
- 1 tablespoon Heavy whipping cream
- 1/2c Coconut flour
- 1/2c Pork rinds
- 1 white Onion

Directions:

1. Warm-up oven to 425. Arrange the first bowl with the coconut flour, the second bowl with mixed whipping cream and beaten egg, and in the third bowl, with crushed pork rinds and grated parmesan cheese, mix.

2. Dip the rings into the coconut flour, then into the egg-cream mixture, and lastly, into the mix of cheese and pork rinds. Bake within fifteen minutes. Serve.

Nutrition:

Calories 205 18g fat 12g protein 4g carbs

99. Cold Crab Dip

Preparation time: 15 minutes

Cooking time: 0 minutes

Servings: 12

Ingredients:

- Lemon juice, 1teaspoon
- Chives, 2tablespoon
- 1/2teaspoon Old Bay seasoning
- Sour cream, 3tablespoon
- 8oz Crabmeat
- 4oz Cream cheese

Directions:

1. Mix the cream cheese, lemon juice, seasoning, and sour cream. Fold the crab meat, then the chives, stirring. Serve.

Nutrition:

Calories 42 4g fat 5g protein

100.   Baked Coconut Shrimp

Preparation time: 15 minutes

Cooking time: 20 minutes

Servings: 4

Ingredients:

- Medium shrimp, 1-pound,
- Black pepper, 1/2teaspoon
- Coconut flakes, 2cups

- Salt, 1/2teaspoon
- Garlic powder, one quarter teaspoon
- Eggs, three
- Paprika, one quarter teaspoon
- Coconut flour, 3tablespoon

Directions:

1. Warm-up oven to 400. In the first bowl, put the beaten eggs, in the second bowl, put the coconut flakes, and in the last bowl, put a mix of the garlic powder, salt, paprika, pepper, and coconut flour.

2. Dip each shrimp into the flour mixture first, then into the egg wash and then roll them in the flakes of coconut. Bake within ten minutes. Serve.

Nutrition:

Calories 440 33 g protein 32 g fat 5 g carbs

101.   Bacon-Wrapped Scallops

Preparation time: 15 minutes

Cooking time: 20 minutes

Servings: 4

Ingredients:

- Toothpicks, 16

- Salt, 1/2 teaspoon
- Olive oil, 2 tablespoon
- Black pepper, 1/2 teaspoon
- Sea scallops
- Bacon

Directions:

1. Warm-up oven to 425. Grease a baking sheet.
2. Use 1/2 of a bacon slice to wrap around each scallop and stick in the toothpick.
3. Brush on the olive oil and put the salt and pepper. Bake within fifteen minutes. Serve.

Nutrition:

Calories 225 13g protein

16g fat 2g carbs

102.   Buffalo Chicken Jalapeno Poppers

Preparation time: 15 minutes

Cooking time: 30 minutes

Servings: 5

Ingredients:

- Ranch dressing
- green onions
- 4 Bacon
- 10 Jalapeno peppers
- Garlic, 2 tablespoon
- Cream cheese, 4oz
- Chicken, 8oz
- Buffalo wing sauce, one quarter cup
- Onion powder, 1/2 teaspoon
- 1/2 cup Blue cheese
- Mozzarella cheese, one quarter cup
- 1/2 teaspoon Salt

Directions:

1. Warm-up oven to 350. Lay the half pieces of the jalapeno peppers on the cookie sheet.
2. Fry the onion powder, ground chicken, garlic, and salt within fifteen minutes.
3. Blend in the mozzarella cheese, wing sauce, and one-quarter cup of the crumbled blue cheese.
4. Combine into the pepper halves, then top with bacon and blue cheese. Bake within thirty minutes then serve.

Nutrition:

Calories 250

15g protein

20g fat

4g carbs

103.   Baked Garlic Parmesan Wings

Preparation time: 15 minutes

Cooking time: 60 minutes

Servings: 6

Ingredients:

- Parsley, 1 tablespoon
- Salt, 1 tablespoon
- Onion powder, 1 teaspoon
- Chicken wings, 2-pounds
- Butter, 1/2 cup
- Parmesan cheese, 1/2 cup
- Garlic powder, 2 teaspoon
- Baking powder, 2 teaspoon
- Black pepper, 1/2 teaspoon

Directions:

1. Warm-up oven to 250. Sprinkle the pepper and salt on the wings and let them sit for ten minutes. Put baking powder over the wings, toss.

2. Bake the wings for thirty minutes. Adjust to 425 F and then bake again for thirty minutes.

3. Meanwhile, mix the minced garlic, parmesan cheese, onion powder, garlic powder, parsley, and melted butter. Toss wings in the sauce. Serve.

Nutrition:

Calories 459

32g protein

40g fat

2g carbs

104. Sausage Stuffed Mushrooms

Preparation time: 15 minutes

Cooking time: 30 minutes

Servings: 20

Ingredients:

- Salt, 1/2teaspoon
- Butter, 2tablespoon
- Sausage, 2
- Garlic, 2teaspoon
- Black pepper, 1/2teaspoon
- Onion, one quarter cup
- Baby Bella Mushrooms, twenty
- Cheddar Cheese, 1cup

Directions:

1. Warm-up oven to 350. Fry sausage meat with butter, remove and put aside.

2. Cook the mushroom stalks, garlic, and diced onion into the pan with the leftover liquid within five minutes.

3. Mix with the salt, cheddar cheese, pepper, and sausage. Fill all of the mushroom caps with this mixture. Bake within twenty minutes. Serve.

Nutrition:

Calories 60

5g protein

4g fat

2g carbs

105. Cheesecake Cupcakes

Preparation time: 10 minutes

Cooking time: 15 minutes

Servings: 12

Ingredients:

- 1 teaspoon vanilla extract
- ½ cup almond meal
- ¾ cup granulated no-calorie sucralose sweetener
- ¼ cup melted butter
- 2 eggs
- 2 8 oz pack softened cream cheese

Directions:

1. Warm-up oven to 350 degrees F.

2. Mix butter and almond meal put into the bottom of the muffin cup.

3. Mix vanilla extract, cream cheese, sucralose sweetener, and egg in an electric mixer. Put this batter to the top of the muffin cups.

4. Bake within 17 minutes. Cool and serve.

Nutrition:

Calories: 209

Carbs: 3.5g

Protein: 4.9g

Fat: 20g

Cholesterol: 82mg

106. Chocolate Peanut Butter Cups

Preparation time: 15 minutes

Cooking time: 3 minutes

Servings: 12

Ingredients:

- 1 oz roasted peanut, salted
- 1 cup of coconut oil
- ¼ teaspoon kosher salt
- ½ cup natural peanut butter
- ¼ teaspoon vanilla extract
- 2 tablespoon heavy cream
- 1 teaspoon liquid stevia
- 1 tablespoon cocoa powder

Directions:

1. Dissolve coconut oil within 5 minutes, then put peanut butter, salt, heavy cream, cocoa powder, vanilla extract, and liquid stevia to the pan. Stir.
2. Put the batter into muffin molds. Put the salted peanuts on top. Chill within an hour. Serve.

Nutrition:

Calories: 246

Carbs: 3.3g

Protein: 3.4g

Fat: 26g

107. Peanut Butter Cookies

Preparation time: 15 minutes

Cooking time: 15 minutes

Servings: 12

Ingredients:

- 1 teaspoon vanilla extract, sugar-free
- 1 cup peanut butter
- 1 egg
- ½ cup natural sweetener, low-calorie

Directions:

1. Heat-up the oven to 350 degrees F.
2. Mix peanut butter, vanilla extract, sweetener, and egg to form a dough.
3. Mold the dough into balls. Bake within 15 minutes. Cool and serve.

Nutrition:

Calories: 133

Carbs: 12.4g

Protein: 5.9g

Fat: 11.2g

108. Low-Carb Almond Coconut Sandies

Preparation time: 15 minutes

Cooking time: 12 minutes

Servings: 18

Ingredients:

- 1/3 teaspoon stevia powder
- 1 cup coconut, unsweetened
- 1 teaspoon Himalayan sea salt
- 1 cup almond meal
- 1 tablespoon vanilla extract
- 1/3 cup melted coconut oil
- 2 tablespoon water
- 1 egg white

Directions:

1. Warm-up oven to 325 F.
2. Mix Himalayan sea salt, unsweetened coconut, stevia powder, almond meal, vanilla extract, coconut oil, water, and egg white. Put aside within 10 minutes.
3. Mold into little balls. Press down on the balls. Bake within 15 minutes. Cool and serve.

Nutrition: Calories: 107   Carbs: 2.7g   Protein: 1.9g   Fat: 10.5g

109. Creme Brulee

Preparation time: 15 minutes

Cooking time: 34 minutes

Servings: 4

Ingredients:

- 5 tablespoon natural sweetener, low calorie
- 4 egg yolks
- 2 cups heavy whipping cream
- 1 teaspoon vanilla extract

Directions:

1. Heat-up the oven to 325 degrees F. Mix the vanilla extract and egg yolks in it.
2. Simmer 1 tablespoon of natural sweetener and heavy cream to the pan and mix. Put the ramekins with batter in a glass baking dish and add hot water.
3. Bake within 30 minutes. Put 1 tablespoon natural sweetener on top. Serve.

Nutrition:

Calorie: 466

Carbs: 16.9g

Protein: 5.1g

Fat: 48.4g

110.   Chocolate Fat Bomb

Preparation time: 15 minutes

Cooking time: 0 minutes

Servings: 10

Ingredients:

- oz pack chocolate pudding mix, sugar-free
- 8 oz package cream cheese
- Coconut oil

Directions:

1. Mix the chocolate pudding mix, cream cheese, and coconut oi using an electric mixer.
2. Put this batter into a mold to form into mounds. Cover and chill within 30 minutes. Serve.

Nutrition:

Calories: 231

Carbs: 3.5g

Protein: 1.9g

Fat: 24.3g

111.   Cocoa Mug Cake

Preparation time: 15 minutes

Cooking time: 5 minutes

Servings: 2

Ingredients:

- 2 tablespoon melted coconut oil
- 6 tablespoon almond flour
- 2 eggs
- 2 tablespoon cocoa powder, unsweetened
- salt
- 2 teaspoon natural sweetener, low-calorie
- ½ teaspoon baking powder

Directions:

1. Mix salt, almond flour, baking powder, cocoa powder, natural sweetener.
2. Beat the eggs using an electric mixer. Put the coconut oil and stir. Put this egg batter into the bowl containing baking powder. Whisk.
3. Put the batter into mugs. Microwave to high within 1 minute. Serve.

Nutrition:

Calories: 338

Carbs: 8.6g

Protein: 12.3g

Fat: 30.9g

CHAPTER 7:

Dinner

112. Baked Fish Fillets with Vegetables in Foil

Preparation time: 15 minutes

Cooking time: 40 minutes

Servings: 3

Ingredients:

- 1 lb. cod
- 1 red bell pepper
- 6 cherry tomatoes
- 1 leek
- ¼ onion
- ½ zucchini
- 1 clove garlic
- 2 tablespoon olives

- 1 oz butter
- 2 tablespoon olive oil
- ½ lemon sliced
- Coriander leaves
- Salt
- pepper

Directions:

1. Warm-up oven to 400°F. Transfer all the vegetables to a baking sheet lined with foil.
2. Cut the fish into bite-sized and add to the vegetables. Add salt and pepper, olive oil and add pieces of butter. Bake for 35 – 40 minutes. Serve.

Nutrition:

Calories 339

Fat 19g

Protein 35g

Carbs 5g

113. Fish & Chips

Preparation time: 15 minutes

Cooking time: 30 minutes

Servings: 2

Ingredients:

For chips:

- ½ tablespoon olive oil
- 1 medium zucchini
- Salt
- pepper

- For fish:
- ¾ lb. cod
- Oil
- ½ cup almond flour
- ¼ teaspoon onion powder

For Sauce:

- 2 tablespoon dill pickle relish
- ¼ tablespoon curry powder
- ½ cup mayonnaise
- ½ teaspoon paprika powder
- ½ cup parmesan cheese
- 1 egg
- Salt
- pepper

Directions:

3. Mix all the sauce fixing in a bowl. Set aside.

4. Warm-up oven to 400°F. Make thin zucchini rods, brush with oil, and spread on the baking sheet. Put salt and pepper then bake within 30 minutes.

5. Beat the egg in a bowl. On a separate plate, combine the parmesan cheese, almond flour, and the remaining spices.

6. Slice the fish into 1 inch by 1-inch pieces. Roll them on the flour mixture. Dip in the beaten egg and then in the flour again. Fry the fish for three minutes. Serve.

Nutrition:

Calories 463

Fat 26.2 g

Protein 49g

Carbs 6g

114. Baked Salmon with Almonds and Cream Sauce

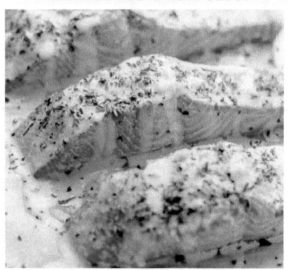

Preparation time: 10 minutes

Cooking time: 20 minutes

Servings: 2

Ingredients:

Almond Crumbs Creamy Sauce

3 tablespoon almonds

2 tablespoon almond milk

½ cup cream cheese

Salt

Fish

1 salmon fillet

1 teaspoon coconut oil

1 tablespoon lemon zest

1 teaspoon salt

White pepper

Directions:

Cut the salmon in half. Rub the salmon with the lemon zest, salt and pepper. Marinade for 20 minutes.

Fry the fish on both sides. Top with almond crumbs and bake within 10 to 15 minutes.

Remove and put aside.

Place the baking dish on fire and add the cream cheese. Combine the fish baking juices and the cheese. Mix, then pour the sauce onto the fish. Serve.

Nutrition:

Calories 522

Fat 44g

Protein 28g

Carbs 2.4g

115. Shrimp and Sausage Bake

Preparation time: 15 minutes

Cooking time: 20 minutes

Servings: 4

Ingredients:

- 2 tablespoon olive oil
- 6 ounces chorizo sausage
- ½ pound shrimp
- ½ small sweet onion
- 1 teaspoon garlic
- ¼ cup Herbed Chicken Stock
- Pinch red pepper flakes
- 1 red bell pepper

Directions:

1. Sauté the sausage within 6 minutes. Add the shrimp and sauté within 4 minutes. Remove both and set aside.
2. Cook the red pepper, onion, and garlic to the skillet within 4 minutes. Put the chicken stock along with the cooked sausage and shrimp. Simmer for 3 minutes.
3. Stir in the red pepper flake and serve.

Nutrition:

Calories 323

Fat 24g

Protein 20g

Carbs 6g

116. Herb Butter Scallops

Preparation time: 10 minutes

Cooking time: 10 minutes

Servings: 4

Ingredients:

- 1-pound sea scallops
- ground black pepper
- 8 tablespoon butter
- 2 teaspoon garlic
- 1 lemon juice
- 2 teaspoon basil
- 1 teaspoon thyme

Directions:

1. Pat dry the scallops then put pepper. Sear each side within 2 ½ minutes per side.
2. Remove then set aside. Sauté the garlic within 3 minutes. Stir in the lemon juice, basil and thyme and return the scallops to the skillet, mix. Serve.

Nutrition:

Calories 306 Fat 24g Protein 19g Carbs 4g

117. Pan-Seared Halibut with Citrus Butter Sauce

Preparation time: 10 minutes

Cooking time: 15 minutes

Servings: 4

Ingredients:

- 4 halibut fillets
- Sea salt
- ground pepper
- ¼ cup butter
- 2 tablespoon garlic
- 1 shallot
- 3 tablespoons dry white wine
- 1 tablespoon orange juice
- 1 tablespoon lemon juice
- 2 teaspoon parsley
- 2 teaspoon olive oil

Directions:

1. Pat dry the fish then put salt and pepper. Set aside.
2. Sauté the garlic and shallot within 3 minutes.
3. Whisk in the white wine, lemon juice, and orange juice and simmer within 2 minutes.
4. Remove the sauce and stir in the parsley; set aside.
5. Panfry the fish until within 10 minutes. Serve with sauce.

Nutrition:

Calories 319

Fat 26g

Protein 22g

Carbs 2g

118. Baked Coconut Haddock

Preparation time: 10 minutes

Cooking time: 12 minutes

Servings: 4

Ingredients:

- 4 (5 oz) boneless haddock fillets
- Sea salt
- Freshly ground pepper
- 1 cup shredded unsweetened coconut
- ½ cup ground hazelnuts
- 2 tablespoon coconut oil, melted

Directions:

1. Warm oven to 400°F.
2. Pat dry fillets and lightly season them with salt and pepper.
3. Stir together the shredded coconut and hazelnut in a small bowl.
4. Dredge the fish fillets in the coconut mixture so that both sides of each piece are thickly coated.
5. Put the fish on the baking sheet and lightly brush both sides of each piece with the coconut oil.

6. Bake the haddock until the topping is golden and the fish flakes easily with a fork, about 12 minutes total. Serve.

Nutrition:

Calories 299 Fat 24g

Protein 20g Carbs 1g

119. Simple Keto Fried Chicken

Preparation time: 15 minutes

Cooking time: 45 minutes

Servings: 4

Ingredients:

- 4 boneless chicken thighs
- Frying oil
- 2 eggs
- 2tablespoon. heavy whipping cream
- Breading
- 2/3cup grated parmesan cheese
- 2/3cup blanched almond flour
- 1teaspoon. salt
- ½teaspoon. black pepper
- ½teaspoon. cayenne
- ½teaspoon. paprika

Directions:

1. Beat the eggs and heavy cream. Separately, mix all the breading fixing. Set aside.

2. Cut the chicken thigh into 3 even pieces.

3. Dip the chicken in the bread first before dipping it in the egg wash and then finally, dipping it in the breading again. Fry chicken within 5 minutes. Pat dry the chicken. Serve.

Nutrition:

Calories: 304 Carbs: 12g Fat: 15g Protein: 30g

120. Keto Butter Chicken

Preparation time: 15 minutes

Cooking time: 20 minutes

Servings: 4

Ingredients:

- 1.5lb. chicken breast
- 1tablespoon. coconut oil
- 2tablespoon. garam masala
- 3teaspoon. grated ginger
- 3teaspoon. garlic
- 4oz. plain yogurt
- Sauce:
- 2tablespoon. butter
- 1tablespoon ground coriander
- ½cup heavy cream

- ½tablespoon. garam masala
- 2teaspoon. ginger
- 2teaspoon. minced garlic
- 2teaspoon. cumin
- 1teaspoon. chili powder
- 1 onion
- 14.5oz. crushed tomatoes
- Salt

Directions:

1. Mix chicken pieces, 2 tablespoons garam masala, 1 teaspoon minced garlic, and 1 teaspoon grated ginger. Stir and add the yogurt. Chill for 30 minutes.

2. For the sauce, blend the ginger, garlic, onion, tomatoes, and spices. Put aside.

3. Cook the chicken pieces. Once cooked, pour in the sauce, and simmer for 5 minutes. Serve.

Nutrition:

Calories: 367 Carbs: 7g Fat: 22g Protein: 36g

121. Keto Shrimp Scampi Recipe

Preparation time: 15 minutes

Cooking time: 25 minutes

Servings: 2

Ingredients:

- 2 summer squash
- 1-pound shrimp
- 2tablespoon. butter unsalted
- 2tablespoon. lemon juice

- 2tablespoon. parsley
- ¼cup chicken broth
- 1/8teaspoon. red chili flakes
- 1 clove garlic
- Salt
- pepper

Directions:

1. Put salt in the squash noodles on top. Set aside for 30 minutes.

2. Pat dry. Fry the garlic. Add some chicken broth, red chili flakes, and lemon juice.

3. Once it boils, add the shrimp, and cook. Lower the heat.

4. Add salt and pepper, put the summer squash noodles and parsley to the mix. Serve.

Nutrition:

Calories: 366 Carbs: 7g Fat: 15g Protein: 49g

122. Keto Lasagna

Preparation time: 15 minutes

Cooking time: 1 hour

Servings: 2

Ingredients:

- 8oz. block cream cheese
- 3 eggs
- Kosher salt

- Ground black pepper
- 2cups mozzarella
- ½cup parmesan
- Pinch red pepper flakes
- parsley
- Sauce:
- ¾cup marinara
- 1tablespoon. tomato paste
- 1lb. ground beef
- ½cup parmesan
- 1.5cup mozzarella
- 1tablespoon. extra virgin olive oil
- 1teaspoon. dried oregano
- 3 cloves garlic
- ½cup onion
- 16oz. ricotta

Directions:

1. Warm-up oven to 350 degrees.
2. Melt in the cream cheese, mozzarella, and parmesan. Put the eggs, salt and pepper.
3. Bake for 15 to 20 minutes.
4. Cook the onion within 5 minutes, then the garlic. Put the tomato paste. Add the ground beef, put salt and pepper. Cook then put aside.
5. Cook marinara sauce, put pepper, red pepper flakes, and ground pepper. Stir.
6. Take out the noodles and cut in half widthwise and then cut them again into 3 pieces.
7. Put 2 noodles at the bottom of the dish, then layer the parmesan and mozzarella shreds alternately.
8. Bake within 30 minutes. Garnish and serve.

Nutrition: Calories: 508 Carbs: 8g

Fat: 39g Protein: 33g

123. Creamy Tuscan Garlic Chicken

Preparation time: 15 minutes

Cooking time: 30 minutes

Servings: 4

Ingredients:

1.5 pounds chicken breast

½cup chicken broth

½cup parmesan cheese

½cup sun-dried tomatoes

1cup heavy cream

1cup spinach

2tablespoon. olive oil

1teaspoon. garlic powder

1teaspoon. Italian seasoning

Directions:

Cook the chicken using olive oil, medium heat within 5 minutes, put aside.

Combine the heavy cream, garlic powder, Italian seasoning, parmesan cheese, and chicken broth. Add the sundried tomatoes and spinach and simmer. Add the chicken back and serve.

Nutrition:

Calories: 368 Carbs: 7g Fat: 0g Protein: 30g

124.   Ancho Macho Chili

Preparation Time: 20 minutes

Cooking Time: 1 hour and 30 minutes

Servings: 4

Ingredients:

- 2lbs. lean sirloin
- Salt 1teaspoon
- Pepper 0.25teaspoon
- Olive Oil 1.5tablespoons
- Onion
- Chili Powder
- 7oz can tomato with green chilis
- ½cup chicken broth
- 2cloves garlic

Directions:

1. Warm-up oven to a temperature of 350F. Coat beef with pepper and salt.

2. Cook a third of the beef. Cook the onion for a few minutes. Put in the last four ingredients and simmer. Add in the beef with all its juices and cook within two hours. Stir and serve.

Nutrition:

Net carbs: 6g

Fat: 40g

Protein: 58g

Calories: 644kcal

125.   Chicken Supreme Pizza

Preparation Time: 25 minutes

Cooking Time: 30 minutes

Servings: 4-8

Ingredients:

- 5oz cooked chicken breast
- Almond Flour 1.5cups
- Baking Powder 1teaspoon
- Salt half-teaspoon - Water 0.25 cup
- Red Onion 1 - Red Pepper 1
- Green Pepper
- Mozzarella Cheese 1cup
- Olive Oil 3tablespoons

Directions:

1. Warm-up oven to a temperature of 400F.

2. Blend the flour both the salt and baking powder. Put the water and the oil added to the flour mixture to make the dough. Flattened dough.

3. Dump out the dough. Press it out, and coat the pan with oil.

4. Bake within 12 minutes. Remove then sprinkle with cheese and then add chicken, pepper, and onion. Bake again within 15 minutes, slice and serve.

Nutrition: Net carbs: 4g Fiber: 10g Fat: 12g Protein: 16g Calories: 310kcal

126.   Baked Jerked Chicken

Preparation Time: 20 minutes

Cooking Time: 1 hour and 30 minutes

Servings: 4

Ingredients:

- 2pounds chicken thighs
- Olive Oil 0.33 cup
- Apple Cider Vinegar
- Salt 1teaspoon
- Powdered Onion 1teaspoon
- garlic half-teaspoon
- Nutmeg half-teaspoon
- Pepper half-teaspoon
- Powdered Ginger half-teaspoon
- Powdered Cayenne half-teaspoon
- Cinnamon 0.25 teaspoon
- Dried Thyme 0.25 teaspoon

Directions:

1. Mix all fixing, excluding the chicken. Stir in the prepared chicken pieces. Stir well.
2. Marinade within 4 hours. Warm-up oven to a temperature of 375F.
3. Cook within 1.25 hours. Adjust to broil chicken within 4 minutes. Serve.

Nutrition:

Net carbs: 4g Fiber: 0g

Fat: 12g Protein: 16g

Calories: 185kcal

127.   Chicken Schnitzel

Preparation Time: 15 minutes

Cooking Time: 15 minutes

Servings: 3

Ingredients:

1. 1-pound chicken breast
2. Almond Flour 0.5 cups
3. Egg 1
4. Powdered Garlic half-tablespoon
5. A powdered onion a half-tablespoon
6. **Keto-Safe Oil**
7. **Directions:**
8. Combine the garlic power flour and onion in a bowl. Separately, beat the egg.
9. With a mallet, pound out the chicken. Put the chicken in the egg mixture. Then roll well through the flour.
10. Take a deep-frying pan and warm-up the oil to medium-high temperature.
11. Add chicken in batches. Fry. Pat dry and serve.

Nutrition:

Net carbs: 32g

Fiber: 0g

Fat: 17g

Protein: 61g

Calories: 541kcl

128. Broccoli and Chicken Casserole

Preparation Time: 15 minutes

Cooking Time: 10 minutes

Servings: 4

Ingredients:

1 ½ lb. chicken breast

8 oz softened cream cheese

Heavy Cream 0.5 cups

Powdered Garlic 1 teaspoon

Powdered Onion 1 teaspoon

Salt half-teaspoon

Pepper half-teaspoon

Broccoli 2 cups, florets

Mozzarella 1 cup

Parmesan 1 cup

Directions:

Warm-up oven to a temperature of 400F.

Combine the cream cheese to pepper and salt. Stir in the cubed chicken.

Put in the baking dish. Put the broccoli into the chicken-cheese mixture.

Top the dish with cheese, bake about 26 minutes and remove. Take off the foil and bake again for 10 minutes. Serve.

Nutrition:

Net carbs: 20g

Fiber: 0g

Fat: 25g

Protein: 21g

Calories: 391kcal

129. Baked Fish with Lemon Butter

Preparation Time: 15 minutes

Cooking Time: 15 minutes

Servings: 2

Ingredients:

- 12 oz white fish fillets
- Olive Oil 1 tablespoon
- Pepper
- Salt
- Broccoli 1 medium-sized
- Butter 2 tablespoons
- Garlic Paste 1 teaspoon
- Lemon 1 medium-sized

Directions:

1. Warm-up the oven to a temperature of 430F.

2. Set the fish out onto the parchment paper, and put pepper and salt. Pour over olive oil and lemon slices. Bake within 15 minutes.

3. Steam the broccoli within five minutes. Put aside.

4. Warm-up, the butter, then stirs in zest, garlic, remaining lemon slices, and broccoli. Cook for 2 minutes before serving.

Nutrition: Net carbs: 1g Fiber: 0g Fat: 15g

Protein: 34g Calories: 276kcal

130.   Chicken Broccoli Alfredo

Preparation Time: 15 minutes

Cooking Time: 10 minutes

Servings: 4

Ingredients:

- Chicken Breast 1 pound
- Spinach 0.5 cups
- Broccoli 1 cup
- Butter 1 tablespoon
- Heavy Cream 0.5 cups
- Garlic 1 clove
- Chopped Onion 2 tablespoons
- ½ teaspoon of salt
- ½ teaspoon of pepper

Directions:

1. Boil broccoli within 10 minutes.
2. Melt the butter with onion and garlic, put the chicken. Sauté within 5 minutes.
3. Put the spinach and broccoli then stir in the cream with seasonings. Cook within 5 minutes and serve.

Nutrition:

Net carbs: 34g Fiber: 0g Fat: 19g

Protein: 34g Calories: 523kcal

131.   Grilled Cheesy Buffalo Chicken

Preparation Time: 15 minutes

Cooking Time: 10 minutes

Servings: 2

Ingredients:

- 10 oz chicken breast
- Garlic 2 cloves
- Mozzarella Cheese 0.25 cup
- Butter 1 tablespoon
- Hot Sauce 0.25 cup
- Lemon Juice 1 tablespoon
- Celery Salt 0.25 teaspoon
- Pepper
- salt

Directions:

1. Mix the minced garlic, hot sauce, celery salt, melted butter, lemon juice, pepper, and salt then put the chicken into the mixture.
2. Fill each chicken breast with cheese. Roll up, then secure with a toothpick to close the pocket.
3. Grease the grill. Cook within 5 minutes, flipping and do another 5 minutes. Nutrition:

Net carbs: 2g

Fiber: 1g

Fat: 5g

Protein: 24g

Calories: 150kcal

132. Middle Eastern Shawarma.

Preparation Time: 15 minutes

Cooking Time: 10 minutes

Servings: 3

Ingredients:

- Lamb Shoulder 1 pound
- Yogurt 2 tablespoons
- Water 1 tablespoon
- White Vinegar 1 teaspoon
- Lemon Juice 2 teaspoons
- Olive Oil 1 teaspoon
- Chopped Onion 2 tablespoons
- Garlic 1 clove
- Black Pepper 0.25 teaspoon
- Cumin 0.25 teaspoon
- Nutmeg 0.25 teaspoon
- Cloves 0.25 teaspoon
- Mace 0.25 teaspoon
- Powdered Cayenne 0.25 teaspoon

Directions:

1. Mix the yogurt to the garlic, put everything else except the lamb. Whisk it.
2. Marinade the lamb strips with this mixture, full day. Set the large skillet to a high temperature. Put the lamb pieces and cook within 5 minutes. Serve.

Nutrition:

Net carbs: 1g Fiber: 0g Fat: 16g Protein: 32g

Calories: 27kcal

133. Tex Mex Casserole

Preparation Time: 15 minutes

Cooking Time: 15 minutes

Servings: 4

Ingredients:

- Sour cream, one cup
- Scallion, one
- Guacamole, one cup
- Leafy greens, one cup
- Ground beef, two pounds
- Tex Mex seasoning three tablespoons
- Monterey Jack cheese one cup
- Jalapenos pickled two ounces
- Crushed Tomatoes seven ounces
- Butter two ounces

Directions:

1. Warm-up oven to 400. Cook the ground beef entirely in the melted butter. Add in the Tex Mex seasoning and the tomatoes and mix well.
2. Put the meat batter in a greased baking pan. Scatter the cheese, and the jalapenos on top, then bake within twenty-five minutes.
3. Chop up the scallion then mix it with the sour cream. Serve the meat mix with a spoon of the sour cream, a scoop of guacamole, and some leafy greens.

Nutrition:

Calories: 860kcal Net carbs: 8g

Fat: 69g Protein: 49g

134. Green Chicken Curry

Preparation time: 15 minutes

Cooking time: 30 minutes

Servings: 4

Ingredients:

- 1-pound grass-fed chicken breasts
- 1tablespoon olive oil
- 2tablespoon green curry paste
- 1cup unsweetened coconut milk
- 1cup chicken broth
- 1cup asparagus spears
- 1cup green beans - Salt
- Ground black pepper
- 1/4 cup basil leaves

Directions:

1. Sauté the curry paste within 1–2 minutes. Add the chicken and cook within 8–10 minutes.
2. Add coconut milk and broth, boil. Cook again to low within 8–10 minutes.
3. Add the asparagus, green beans, salt, and black pepper, and cook within 4–5 minutes.

Nutrition: Calories 294 Net Carbs 4.3 g

Total Fat 16.2 g Protein 28.6 g

Preparation time: 15 minutes

Cooking time: 1 hour 35 minutes

Servings: 8

Ingredients:

- 3tablespoon unsalted butter
- 2½ pounds boneless pork ribs
- 1 yellow onion
- 4 garlic cloves
- 1½cups chicken broth
- 2cans sugar-free diced tomatoes
- 2teaspoon dried oregano
- 1teaspoon ground cumin
- Salt
- 2tablespoon lime juice
- ½cup sour cream

Directions:

1. Cook the pork, onions, and garlic within 4–5 minutes. Add the broth, tomatoes, oregano, cumin, and salt, and mix. Simmer to low.
2. Combine in the sour cream plus lime juice and remove. Serve.

Nutrition:

Calories 304 Net Carbs 4.7 g Total Fat 12.4 g

Protein 39.5 g

---

135. Creamy Pork Stew

136. Salmon & Shrimp Stew

Preparation time: 20 minutes

Cooking time: 25 minutes

Servings: 6

Ingredients:

- 2tablespoon coconut oil
- ½cup onion
- 2 garlic cloves
- 1 Serrano pepper
- 1teaspoon smoked paprika

- 24cups tomatoes
- 4cups chicken broth
- 1-pound salmon fillets
- 1-pound shrimp
- 2tablespoon lime juice
- Salt
- ground black pepper
- 3 tablespoons parsley

Directions:

1. Sauté the onion within 5–6 minutes. Add the garlic, Serrano pepper, and paprika. Add the tomatoes and broth then boil.
2. Simmer within 5 minutes. Add the salmon and simmer again, 3–4 minutes.
3. Put in the shrimp then cook within 4–5 minutes. Mix in lemon juice, salt plus black pepper, and remove. Serve with parsley.

Nutrition: Calories 247 Net Carbs 3.9 g

Fiber 1.2 g Sugar 2.1 g Protein 32.7 g

137. Chicken Casserole

Preparation time: 15 minutes

Cooking time: 1 hour 10 minutes

Servings: 6

Ingredients:

- Chicken Layer
- 6 grass-fed chicken breasts
- Salt
- ground black pepper
- Bacon Layer
- 5 bacon slices
- ¼cup yellow onion
- ¼cup jalapeño pepper
- ½cup mayonnaise
- 1package cream cheese
- ½cup Parmesan cheese
- 1cup cheddar cheese

Topping

- 1 package pork skins
- ¼cup butter
- ½cup Parmesan cheese

Directions:

1. Warm-up oven to 4250F.
2. Put the chicken breasts in the greased casserole then put salt and black pepper.
3. Bake within 30–40 minutes.
4. For the bacon layer:
5. Cook the bacon within 8–10 minutes. Transfer.
6. Sauté onion within 4–5 minutes. Remove, stir in bacon and remaining fixing.
7. Remove the casserole dish then put the bacon mixture.
8. Mix all topping fixing. Place the topping over the bacon mixture. Bake within 15 minutes. Serve.

Nutrition:

Calories 826 Net Carbs 2.5 g

Total Fat 62.9 g Protein 60.6 g

138. Creamy Chicken Bake

Preparation time: 15 minutes

Cooking time: 1 hour 10 minutes

Servings: 6

Ingredients:

- 5tablespoon unsalted butter
- 2 onions
- 3 garlic cloves
- 1teaspoon tarragon
- 8oz cream cheese
- 1cup chicken broth
- 2tablespoon lemon juice
- ½cup heavy cream
- 1½teaspoons Herbs de Provence
- Salt
- ground black pepper
- 4 grass-fed chicken breasts

Directions:

1. Warm-up oven to 3500F.
2. Cook the onion, garlic, and tarragon within 4–5 minutes. Transfer.
3. Cook the cream cheese, ½ cup of broth, and lemon juice within 3–4 minutes.

4. Stir in the cream, herbs de Provence, salt, and black pepper, remove.
5. Pour remaining broth and chicken breast plus the cream mixture. Bake within 45–60 minutes. Serve.

Nutrition:

Calories 729

Net Carbs 5.6 g

Total Fat 52.8 g

Sugar 2 g

Protein 55.8 g

139. Beef & Veggie Casserole

Preparation time: 20 minutes

Cooking time: 55 minutes

Servings: 6

Ingredients:

- 3tablespoon butter
- 1-pound grass-fed ground beef
- 1 yellow onion
- 2 garlic cloves
- 1cup pumpkin
- 1cup broccoli
- 2cups cheddar cheese
- 1tablespoon Dijon mustard
- 6 organic eggs
- ½cup heavy whipping cream

- Salt
- ground black pepper

Directions:

1. Cook the beef within 8–10 minutes. Transfer.

2. Cook the onion and garlic within 10 minutes. Add the pumpkin and cook within 5–6 minutes.

3. Add the broccoli and cook within 3–4 minutes. Transfer to the cooked beef, combine.

4. Warm-up oven to 350°F.

5. Put 2/3 of cheese and mustard in the beef mixture, combine.

6. In another mixing bowl, add cream, eggs, salt, and black pepper, and beat.

7. In a baking dish, place the beef mixture and top with egg mixture, plus the remaining cheese.

8. Bake within 25 minutes. Serve.

Nutrition:

Calories 472

Net Carbs 5.5 g

Total Fat 34.6 g

Sodium 463 mg

Protein 32.6 g

140.   Beef with Bell Peppers

Preparation time: 15 minutes

Cooking time: 10 minutes

Servings: 4

Ingredients:

- 1tablespoon olive oil
- 1-pound grass-fed flank steak
- 1 red bell pepper
- 1 green bell pepper
- 1tablespoon ginger
- 3tablespoon low-sodium soy sauce

- 1½tablespoon balsamic vinegar
- 2teaspoon Sriracha

Directions:

1. Sear the steak slices within 2 minutes. Cook bell peppers within 2–3 minutes.

2. Transfer the beef mixture. Boil the remaining fixing within 1 minute. Add the beef mixture and cook within 1–2 minutes. Serve.

Nutrition:

Calories 274

Net Carbs 3.8 g

Total Fat 13.1 g

Protein 32.9 g

141.   Braised Lamb shanks

Preparation time: 15 minutes

Cooking time: 2 hours 35 minutes

Servings: 4

Ingredients:

- 4 grass-fed lamb shanks
- 2tablespoon butter
- Salt
- ground black pepper
- 6 garlic cloves

- 6 rosemary sprigs
- 1cup chicken broth

Directions:

1. Warm-up oven to 450°F.
2. Coat the shanks with butter and put salt plus pepper. Roast within 20 minutes.
3. Remove then reduce to 325°F.
4. Place the garlic cloves and rosemary over and around the lamb.
5. Roast within 2 hours. Put the broth into a roasting pan.
6. Increase to 400°F. Roast within 15 minutes more. Serve.

Nutrition:

Calories 1093

Net Carbs 2 g

Total Fat 44.2 g

Protein 161.4 g

142. Shrimp & Bell Pepper Stir-Fry

Preparation time: 20 minutes

Cooking time: 10 minutes

Servings: 6

Ingredients:

- ½cup low-sodium soy sauce
- 2tablespoons balsamic vinegar
- 2tablespoons Erythritol
- 1tablespoon arrowroot starch
- 1tablespoon ginger

- ½teaspoon red pepper flakes
- 3tablespoons olive oil
- ½ red bell pepper
- ½ yellow bell pepper
- ½ green bell pepper
- 1 onion
- 1 red chili
- 1½ pounds shrimp
- 2 scallion greens

Directions:

1. Mix soy sauce, vinegar, erythritol, arrowroot starch, ginger, and red pepper flakes. Set aside.
2. Stir-fry the bell peppers, onion, and red chili within 1–2 minutes.
3. In the center of the wok, place the shrimp and cook within 1–2 minutes.
4. Stir the shrimp with bell pepper mixture and cook within 2 minutes.
5. Stir in the sauce and cook within 2–3 minutes.
6. Stir in the scallion greens and remove. Serve hot.

Nutrition:

Calories 221

Net Carbs 6.5 g

Total Fat 9 g

Protein 27.6 g

143. Low Carb Beef Stir Fry

Preparation time: 15 minutes

Cooking time: 20 minutes

Servings: 4

Ingredients:

- ½cup zucchini
- ¼cup organic broccoli florets
- 1 baby book Choy

- 2tablespoon. avocado oil
- 2teaspoon. coconut amines
- 1 ginger
- 8oz. skirt steak

Directions:

1. Sear the steak on high heat. Adjust to medium and put in the broccoli, ginger, ghee, and coconut amines. Add in the book Choy and cook for another minute.
2. Put the zucchini into the mix and cook. Serve.

Nutrition:

Calories: 275

Carbs: 12g

Fat: 5g

Protein: 40g

144. Veggies & Walnut Loaf

Preparation time: 15 minutes

Cooking time: 1 hour 10 minutes

Servings: 10

Ingredients:

- 1tablespoon olive oil
- 2 yellow onions
- 2 garlic cloves
- 1teaspoon dried rosemary
- 1cup walnuts
- 2 carrots
- 1 celery stalk
- 1 green bell pepper
- 1cup button mushrooms
- 5 organic eggs
- 1¼cups almond flour
- Salt
- ground black pepper

Directions:

1. Warm-up oven to 350°F. Sauté the onion within 4–5 minutes.
2. Add the garlic and rosemary and sauté within 1 minute.
3. Add the walnuts and vegetables within 3–4 minutes. Put aside
4. Beat the eggs, flour, sea salt, and black pepper.
5. Mix the egg mixture with vegetable mixture.
6. Bake within 50–60 minutes. Serve.

Nutrition:

Calories 242 Net Carbs 4.6 g Total Fat 19.5 g

Protein 5.9 g

145. One Pan Pesto Chicken and Veggies

Preparation time: 15 minutes

Cooking time: 25 minutes

Servings: 4

Ingredients:

- 2tablespoon. olive oil
- 1cup cherry diced tomatoes
- ¼cup basil pesto
- 1/3cup sun-dried tomatoes
- 1-pound chicken thigh

- 1-pound asparagus

Directions:

1. Warm-up a large skillet. Put two tablespoons of olive oil and sliced chicken on medium heat. Put salt and add ½ cup of the sun-dried tomatoes. Cook. Transfer the chicken and tomatoes.

2. Put the asparagus in the skillet and pour it in the pesto. Put the remaining sun-dried tomatoes. Cook within 5 to 10 minutes. Transfer.

3. Turn the chicken back in the skillet and pour it in pesto. Stir for 2 minutes. Serve with the asparagus.

Nutrition:

Calories: 340 Carbs: 9g Fat: 24g Protein: 23g

146. Crispy Peanut Tofu and Cauliflower Rice Stir-Fry

Preparation time: 15 minutes

Cooking time: 1 hour

Servings: 4

Ingredients:

- 12oz. tofu

- 1tablespoon. toasted sesame oil

- 2cloves minced garlic

- 1 cauliflower head

- Sauce

- 1 ½tablespoon. Toasted sesame oil

- ½teaspoon. chili garlic sauce

- 2 ½tablespoon. peanut butter

- ¼cup low sodium soy sauce

- ½cup light brown sugar

Directions:

1. Warm-up oven to 400 degrees. Cube the tofu.

2. Bake for 25 minutes and cool.

3. Combine the sauce fixing. Put the tofu in the sauce and stir. Leave for 15 minutes.

4. Cook the veggies on a bit of sesame oil and soy sauce. Set it aside.

5. Grab the tofu and put it on the pan. Stir then set aside.

6. Steam the cauliflower rice for 5 to 8 minutes. Add some sauce and stir.

7. Add up the ingredients. Put the cauliflower rice with the veggies and tofu. Serve.

Nutrition:

Calories: 524 Carbs: 39g Fat: 34g Protein: 25g

147. Low Carb Crack Slaw Egg Roll in a Bowl Recipe

Preparation time: 15 minutes

Cooking time: 20 minutes

Servings: 2

Ingredients:

- 1lb. ground beef

- 4cups shredded coleslaw mix

- 1tablespoon. avocado oil

- 1teaspoon. Sea salt
- ¼teaspoon. black pepper
- 4cloves garlic
- 3tablespoon. ginger
- ¼cup coconut amines
- 2teaspoon. toasted sesame oil
- ¼cup green onions

Directions:

1. Warm-up avocado oil in a large pan, put in the garlic, and cook.
2. Add the ground beef and cook within 10 minutes, put salt and black pepper.
3. Lower the heat and add the coleslaw mix and the coconut amines. Stir to cook for 5 minutes.
4. Remove and put in the green onions and the toasted sesame oil. Serve.

Nutrition:

Calories: 116

Carbs: 2g

Fat: 13g

Protein: 8g

148.   Keto Sloppy Joes

Preparation time: 15 minutes

Cooking time: 1 hour 10 minutes

Servings: 3

Ingredients:

- 1 ¼cup almond flour

- 5tablespoon. ground psyllium husk powder
- 1teaspoon. sea salt
- 2teaspoon. baking powder
- 2teaspoon. cider vinegar
- 1 ¼ cups boiling water
- 3 egg whites
- 2tablespoon. olive oil
- 1 ½ lb. ground beef
- 1 yellow onion
- 4 garlic cloves
- 14oz. crushed tomatoes
- 1tablespoon. chili powder
- 1tablespoon. Dijon powder
- 1tablespoon. red wine vinegar
- 4tablespoon. tomato paste
- 2teaspoon. salt
- ¼teaspoon ground black pepper
- ½cup mayonnaise
- 6oz. cheese

Directions:

1. Warm-up the oven to 350 degrees and then mix all the dry fixing.
2. Add some vinegar, egg whites, and boiled water. Whisk for 30 seconds.
3. Form the dough into 5 or 8 pieces of bread. Cook within 55 minutes.
4. Cook the onion and garlic. Add the ground beef and cook. Put the other fixing and cook. Simmer for 10 minutes in low. Serve.

Nutrition:

Calories: 215

Carbs: 19g

Fat: 10g

Protein: 30g

149. Spicy Steak Curry

Preparation Time: 15 minutes

Cooking Time: 40 minutes

Servings: 6

Ingredients:

- 1 cup plain yogurt
- ½ teaspoon garlic paste
- ½ teaspoon ginger paste
- ½ teaspoon ground cloves
- ½ teaspoon ground cumin
- 2 teaspoons red pepper flakes
- ¼ teaspoon ground turmeric
- Salt
- 2 pounds grass-fed round steak
- ¼ cup olive oil
- 1 medium yellow onion
- 1½ tablespoons lemon juice
- ¼ cup cilantro

Directions:

1. Mix yogurt, garlic paste, ginger paste and spices. Add the steak pieces. Set aside.
2. Sauté the onion within 4-5 minutes. Add the steak pieces with marinade and mix.

3. Simmer within 25 minutes. Stir in the lemon juice and simmer 10 minutes.
4. Garnish with cilantro and serve.

Nutrition:

Calories: 440

Net Carbs: 4.8g

Carbohydrate: 5.5g

Fiber: 0.7g

Protein: 48.3g

150. Beef Stew

Preparation Time: 15 minutes

Cooking Time: 1 hour 40 minutes

Servings: 4

Ingredients:

- 1 1/3 pounds grass-fed chuck roast
- Salt
- ground black pepper
- 2 tablespoons butter
- 1 yellow onion
- 2 garlic cloves
- 1 cup beef broth
- 1 bay leaf
- ½ teaspoon dried thyme
- ½ teaspoon dried rosemary
- 1 carrot
- 4 ounces celery stalks
- 1 tablespoon lemon juice

Directions:

1. Put salt and black pepper in beef cubes.
2. Sear the beef cubes within 4-5 minutes. Add the onion and garlic, then adjust the heat to medium and cook within 4-5 minutes. Add the broth, bay leaf and dried herbs and boil.

3. Simmer within 45 minutes. Stir in the carrot and celery and simmer within 30-45 minutes.

4. Stir in lemon juice, salt, and black pepper. Serve.

Nutrition:

Calories: 413

Net Carbs: 4.3g

Carbohydrate: 5.9g

Fiber: 1.6g

Protein: 52g

151.   Beef & Cabbage Stew

Preparation Time: 15 minutes

Cooking Time: 2 hours 10 minutes

Servings: 8

Ingredients:

- 2 pounds grass-fed beef stew meat
- 1 1/3 cups hot chicken broth
- 2 yellow onions
- 2 bay leaves
- 1 teaspoon Greek seasoning
- Salt
- ground black pepper
- 3 celery stalks

- 1 package cabbage
- 1 can sugar-free tomato sauce
- 1 can sugar-free whole plum tomatoes

Directions:

1. Sear the beef within 4-5 minutes. Stir in the broth, onion, bay leaves, Greek seasoning, salt, and black pepper and boil. Adjust the heat to low and cook within 1¼ hours.

2. Stir in the celery and cabbage and cook within 30 minutes. Stir in the tomato sauce and chopped plum tomatoes and cook, uncovered within 15-20 minutes.

3. Stir in the salt, discard bay leaves and serve.

Nutrition:

Calories: 247

Net Carbs: 4.9g

Carbohydrate: 7g

Fiber: 2.1g

Protein: 36.5g

152.   Beef & Mushroom Chili

Preparation Time: 15 minutes

Cooking Time: 3 hours 10 minutes

Servings: 8

Ingredients:

- 2 pounds grass-fed ground beef
- 1 yellow onion
- ½ cup green bell pepper
- ½ cup carrot
- 4 ounces mushrooms
- 2 garlic cloves
- 1 can sugar-free tomato paste
- 2 tablespoons red chili powder
- 1 tablespoon ground cumin
- 1 teaspoon ground cinnamon

- 1 teaspoon red pepper flakes
- ½ teaspoon ground allspice
- Salt
- ground black pepper
- 4 cups of water
- ½ cup sour cream

Directions:

1. Cook the beef within 8-10 minutes. Stir in the remaining fixing except for sour cream and boil. Cook on low, covered, within 3 hours. Top with sour cream and serve.

Nutrition:

Calories: 246

Net Carbs: 5.9g

Carbohydrate: 8.2g

Fiber: 2.3g

Protein: 25.1g

153. Steak with Cheese Sauce

Preparation Time: 15 minutes

Cooking Time: 17 minutes

Servings: 4

Ingredients:

- 18 ounces grass-fed filet mignon
- Salt

- ground black pepper
- 2 tablespoons butter
- ½ cup yellow onion
- 5¼ ounces blue cheese
- 1 cup heavy cream
- 1 garlic clove
- ground nutmeg

Directions:

1. Cook onion within 5-8 minutes. Add the blue cheese, heavy cream, garlic, nutmeg, salt, and black pepper and stir.
2. Cook for about 3-5 minutes.
3. Put salt and black pepper in filet mignon steaks. Cook the steaks within 4 minutes per side.
4. Transfer and set aside. Top with cheese sauce, then serve.

Nutrition:

Calories: 521

Net Carbs: 3g

Carbohydrate: 3.3g

Fiber: 0.3g

Protein: 44.7g

154. Steak with Blueberry Sauce

Preparation Time: 15 minutes

Cooking Time: 20 minutes

Servings: 4

Ingredients:

For Sauce:

- 2 tablespoons butter
- 2 tablespoons yellow onion
- 2 garlic cloves
- 1 teaspoon thyme
- 1 1/3 cups beef broth

- 2 tablespoons lemon juice
- ¾ cup blueberries

For Steak:

- 2 tablespoons butter
- 4 grass-fed flank steaks
- Salt
- ground black pepper

Directions:

1. For the sauce: sauté the onion within 2-3 minutes.
2. Add the garlic and thyme and sauté within 1 minute. Stir in the broth and simmer within 10 minutes.
3. For the steak: put salt and black pepper. Cook steaks within 3-4 minutes per side.
4. Transfer and put aside. Add sauce in the skillet and stir. Stir in the lemon juice, blueberries, salt, and black pepper and cook within 1-2 minutes. Put blueberry sauce over the steaks. Serve.

Nutrition:

Calories: 467 Net Carbs: 4.6g Fiber: 0.9g

Protein: 49.5g

155.   Grilled Steak

Preparation Time: 15 minutes

Cooking Time: 12 minutes

Servings: 6

Ingredients:

- 1 teaspoon lemon zest
- 1 garlic clove
- 1 tablespoon red chili powder
- 1 tablespoon paprika
- 1 tablespoon ground coffee
- Salt
- ground black pepper
- 2 grass-fed skirt steaks

Directions:

1. Mix all the ingredients except steaks. Marinate the steaks and keep aside within 30-40 minutes.
2. Grill the steaks within 5-6 minutes per side. Remove then cool before slicing. Serve.

Nutrition: Calories: 473 Net Carbs: 0.7g

Carbohydrate: 1.6g Fiber: 0.9g Protein: 60.8g

156.   Roasted Tenderloin

Preparation Time: 10 minutes

Cooking Time: 50 minutes

Servings: 10

Ingredients:

- 1 grass-fed beef tenderloin roast

- 4 garlic cloves
- 1 tablespoon rosemary
- Salt
- ground black pepper
- 1 tablespoon olive oil

Directions:

1. Warm-up oven to 425 degrees F.
2. Place beef meat into the prepared roasting pan. Massage with garlic, rosemary, salt, and black pepper and oil. Roast the beef within 45-50 minutes.
3. Remove, cool, slice and serve.

Nutrition:

Calories: 295

Net Carbs: 0.4g

Fiber: 0.2g

Protein: 39.5g

Fat: 13.9g

157. Garlicky Prime Rib Roast

Preparation Time: 15 minutes

Cooking Time: 1 hour 35 minutes

Servings: 15

Ingredients:

- 10 garlic cloves
- 2 teaspoons dried thyme
- 2 tablespoons olive oil

- Salt
- ground black pepper
- 1 grass-fed prime rib roast

Directions:

1. Mix the garlic, thyme, oil, salt, and black pepper. Marinate the rib roast with garlic mixture within 1 hour.
2. Warm-up oven to 500 degrees F.
3. Roast within 20 minutes. Lower to 325 degrees F and roast within 65-75 minutes.
4. Remove then cool down within 10-15 minutes, slice and serve.

Nutrition:

Calories: 499

Net Carbs: 0.6g

Carbohydrate: 0.7g

Fiber: 0.1g

Protein: 61.5g

Fat: 25.9g

158. Beef Taco Bake

Preparation Time: 15 minutes

Cooking Time: 1 hour

Servings: 6

Ingredients:

For Crust:

- 3 organic eggs
- 4 ounces cream cheese
- ½ teaspoon taco seasoning
- 1/3 cup heavy cream
- 8 ounces cheddar cheese

For Topping:

- 1-pound grass-fed ground beef
- 4 ounces green chilies
- ¼ cup sugar-free tomato sauce
- 3 teaspoons taco seasoning
- 8 ounces cheddar cheese

Directions:

1. Warm-up oven to 375 degrees F.
2. For the crust: beat the eggs, and cream cheese, taco seasoning, and heavy cream.
3. Place cheddar cheese in the baking dish. Spread cream cheese mixture over cheese.
4. Bake within 25-30 minutes. Remove then set aside within 5 minutes.
5. For topping:
6. Cook the beef within 8-10 minutes.
7. Stir in the green chilies, tomato sauce, and taco seasoning and transfer.
8. Place the beef mixture over the crust and sprinkle with cheese. Bake within 18-20 minutes.
9. Remove then slice and serve.

Nutrition:

Calories: 569

Net Carbs: 3.8g

Carbohydrate: 4g

Fiber: 0.2g

Protein: 38.7g

159. Chocolate Chili

Preparation Time: 15 minutes

Cooking Time: 2¼ hours

Servings: 8

Ingredients:

- 2 tablespoons olive oil
- 1 small onion
- 1 green bell pepper
- 4 garlic cloves
- 1 jalapeño pepper
- 1 teaspoon dried thyme
- 2 tablespoons red chili powder
- 1 tablespoon ground cumin
- 2 pounds lean ground pork
- 2 cups fresh tomatoes
- 4 ounces sugar-free tomato paste
- 1½ tablespoons cacao powder
- 2 cups chicken broth
- 1 cup of water
- Salt
- ground black pepper
- ¼ cup cheddar cheese,

Directions:

1. Sauté the onion and bell pepper within 5-7 minutes.
2. Add the garlic, jalapeño pepper, thyme, and spices and sauté within 1 minute.
3. Add the pork and cook within 4-5 minutes. Stir in the tomatoes, tomato paste, and cacao powder and cook within 2 minutes.
4. Add the broth and water, boil. Simmer, covered within 2 hours. Stir in the salt and black pepper. Remove then top with cheddar cheese and serve.

Nutrition:

Calories: 326

Net Carbs: 6.5g

Carbohydrate: 9.1g

Fiber: 2.6g

Protein: 23.3g

Fat: 22.9g

160.   Pork Stew

Preparation Time: 15 minutes

Cooking Time: 45 minutes

Servings: 6

Ingredients:

- 2 tablespoons olive oil
- 2 pounds pork tenderloin
- 1 tablespoon garlic
- 2 teaspoons paprika
- ¾ cup chicken broth
- 1 cup sugar-free tomato sauce
- ½ tablespoon Erythritol
- 1 teaspoon dried oregano
- 2 dried bay leaves
- 2 tablespoons lemon juice
- Salt
- ground black pepper

Directions:

1. Cook the pork within 3-4 minutes. Add the garlic and cook within 1 minute.
2. Stir in the remaining fixing and boil. Simmer, covered within 30-40 minutes
3. Remove then discard the bay leaves. Serve.

Nutrition:

Calories: 277

Net Carbs: 2.5g

Carbohydrate: 3.6g

Fiber: 1.1g

Protein: 41g

Fat: 10.4g

161.   Pork & Chiles Stew

Preparation Time: 15 minutes

Cooking Time: 2 hours & 10 minutes

Servings: 8

Ingredients

- 3 tablespoons unsalted butter
- 2½ pounds boneless pork ribs
- 1 large yellow onion
- 4 garlic cloves
- 1½ cups chicken broth
- 2 cans sugar-free tomatoes
- 1 cup canned roasted poblano chilies
- 2 teaspoons dried oregano
- 1 teaspoon ground cumin
- Sal
- ¼ cup cilantro
- 2 tablespoons lime juice

Directions:

1. Cook the pork, onions and garlic within 5 minutes.
2. Add the broth, tomatoes, poblano chilies, oregano, cumin, and salt and boil.
3. Simmer, covered within 2 hours. Mix with the fresh cilantro and lime juice and remove it. Serve.

Nutrition Values: Calories: 288 Net Carbs:6g Carbohydrate: 8.8g Fiber: 2.8g Protein: 39.6g

CHAPTER 8:

Vegetarians

162.   Berries & Spinach Salad

Preparation time: 10 minutes

Cooking time: 0 minutes

Servings: 5

Ingredients:

Salad

- 8 cups fresh baby spinach
- ¾ cup fresh strawberries, hulled and sliced
- ¾ cup fresh blueberries
- ¼ cup onion, sliced
- ¼ cup almond, sliced
- ¼ cup feta cheese, crumbled

Dressing

- 1/3 cup olive oil
- 2 tablespoons fresh lemon juice
- ¼ teaspoon liquid stevia
- 1/8 teaspoon garlic powder
- Salt, to taste

Directions:

4. For salad: In a bowl, add the spinach, berries, onion, and almonds, and mix.

5. For dressing: In another small bowl, add all the ingredients and beat until well combined.

6. Place the dressing over salad and gently, toss to coat well.

Nutrition:

Calories 190 Net Carbs 6 g

Total Fat 17.2 g Saturated Fat 3.3 g

Cholesterol 7 mg

Sodium 145 mg Total Carbs 8.5 g

Fiber 2.5 g Sugar 4.6 g

Protein 3.3 g

163.   Egg & Avocado Salad

Preparation time: 10 minutes

Cooking time: 0 minutes

Servings: 4

Ingredients:

Dressing

- 3 tablespoons olive oil
- 1 tablespoon fresh lime juice
- Salt and ground black pepper, to taste

Salad

- 5 cups fresh baby greens
- 4 hard-boiled organic eggs, peeled and sliced
- 2 avocados; peeled, pitted, and sliced
- 2 tablespoons fresh mint leaves

Directions:

7. For dressing: Place oil, lime juice, salt, and black pepper in a small bowl and beat until well combined.
8. Divide the spinach onto serving plates and top each with tuna, egg, cucumber, and tomato.
9. Drizzle with dressing and serve.

Nutrition:

Calories 332

Net Carbs 2.5 g

Total Fat 31.5 g

Saturated Fat 6.4 g

Cholesterol 164 mg

Sodium 111 mg

Total Carbs 8.8 g

Fiber 6.3 g

Sugar 1.2 g

Protein 7.7 g

164. Tomato, Arugula & Mozzarella Salad

Preparation time: 15 minutes

Cooking time: 0 minutes

Servings: 4

Ingredients:

Dressing

- ½ cup fresh basil leaves
- 2 garlic cloves, peeled
- 4 tablespoons olive oil
- 2 tablespoon balsamic vinegar
- Salt and ground black pepper, to taste

Salad

- 2 cups cherry tomatoes
- 3 ounces mozzarella cheese balls
- 5 cups fresh arugula

Directions:

1. For filling: In a small blender, add all the ingredients and pulse until smooth.
2. For salad: In a large bowl, add all the ingredients and mix.
3. Place the dressing over salad and toss to coat well.
4. Serve immediately.

Nutrition:

Calories 207

Net Carbs 4.2 g

Total Fat 18.1 g

Saturated Fat 4.3 g

Cholesterol 11 mg

Sodium 178 mg

Total Carbs 5.8 g

Fiber 1.6 g

Sugar 2.9 g

Protein 7.6 g

165. Smoked Salmon & Zucchini Salad

Preparation time: 10 minutes

Cooking time: 0 minutes

Servings: 4

Ingredients:

Dressing

- 3 tablespoons olive oil
- 2 tablespoons balsamic vinegar
- ½ tablespoon Dijon mustard
- ¼ teaspoon red pepper flakes, crushed

Salad

- 12 ounces smoked salmon
- 3 medium zucchinis, spiralized with blade C
- 1 cup fresh mozzarella balls
- 2 tablespoons fresh basil, chopped

Directions:

1. For dressing: In a small blender, add all the ingredients and pulse until smooth.

2. For salad: In a large bowl, add all the ingredients and mix.

3. Place the dressing over salad and toss to coat well.

4. Serve immediately.

Nutrition:

Calories 158

Net Carbs 2.4 g

Total Fat 10.5 g

Saturated Fat 2.1 g

Cholesterol 16 mg

Sodium 1,100 mg

Total Carbs 3.6 g

Fiber 1.2 g

Sugar 1.7 g

Protein 13 g

166. Cucumber & Tomato Salad

Preparation time: 15 minutes

Cooking time: 0 minutes

Servings: 4

Ingredients:

- Salad
- 3 large English cucumbers, thinly sliced
- 2 cups tomatoes, chopped
- 6 cups lettuce, torn
- Dressing
- 4 tablespoons olive oil
- 2 tablespoons balsamic vinegar
- 1 tablespoon fresh lemon juice
- Salt and ground black pepper, as required

Directions:

1. For salad: In a large bowl, add the cucumbers, onion, cucumbers, and mix.

2. For dressing: In a small bowl, add all the ingredients and beat until well combined.

3. Place the dressing over the salad and toss to coat well.

4. Serve immediately.

Nutrition:

Calories 86

Net Carbs 0 g

Total Fat 7.3 g

Saturated Fat 1 g

Cholesterol 0 mg

Sodium 27 mg

Total Carbs 5.1 g

Fiber 1.4 g

Sugar 2.8 g

Protein 1.1 g

167.   Creamy Shrimp Salad

Preparation time: 15 minutes

Cooking time: 0 minutes

Servings: 4

Ingredients:

- ¼ cup sour cream
- 2 tablespoons mayonnaise
- 2 tablespoons fresh lemon juice
- 1 teaspoon Old Bay seasoning
- Salt, to taste
- 16 ounces cooked shrimp

- 2 medium cucumbers, peeled and chopped
- 3 tablespoons fresh parsley, chopped

Directions:

1. Add sour cream, mayonnaise, lime juice, Old Bay, and salt in a large salad bowl and mix well.

2. Add remaining ingredients and gently, stir to combine.

3. Refrigerate to chill before serving.

Nutrition:

Calories 225

Net Carbs 4.9 g

Total Fat 10.1 g

Saturated Fat 3.3 g

Cholesterol 248 mg

Sodium 533 mg

Total Carbs 5.4 g

Fiber 0.5 g

Sugar 1.5 g

Protein 26.9 g

168.   Salmon Salad

Preparation time: 20 minutes

Cooking time: 0 minutes

Servings: 4

Ingredients:

- 12 hard-boiled organic eggs, peeled and cubed
- 1 pound smoked salmon

- 3 celery stalks, chopped
- 1 yellow onion, chopped
- 4 tablespoons fresh dill, chopped
- 2 cups mayonnaise
- Salt and ground black pepper, as required
- 8 cups fresh lettuce leaves

Directions:

1. In a large serving bowl, add all the ingredients (except the lettuce leaves) and gently stir to combine.

2. Cover and refrigerate to chill before serving. Divide the lettuce onto serving plates and top with the salmon salad.

3. Serve immediately.

Nutrition:

Calories 539 Net Carbs 3.5 g

Total Fat 49.2 g Saturated Fat 8.6 g

Cholesterol 279 mg Sodium 1618 mg

Total Carbs 4.5 g Fiber 1 g Sugar 1.7 g

Protein 19.4 g

169.   Chicken & Strawberry Salad

Preparation time: 15 minutes

Cooking time: 0 minutes

Servings: 4

Ingredients:

- 2 pounds grass-fed boneless skinless chicken breasts

- ½ cup olive oil
- ¼ cup fresh lemon juice
- 2 tablespoons granulated erythritol
- 1 garlic clove, minced
- Salt and ground black pepper, as required
- 4 cups fresh strawberries
- 8 cups fresh spinach, torn

Directions:

1. For marinade: in a large bowl, add oil, lemon juice, erythritol, garlic, salt, and black pepper, and beat until well combined.

2. In a large resealable plastic bag, place the chicken and ¾ cup of marinade.

3. Seal bag and shake to coat well.

4. Refrigerate overnight.

5. Cover the bowl of remaining marinade and refrigerate before serving.

6. Preheat the grill to medium heat. Grease the grill grate.

7. Remove the chicken from bag and discard the marinade.

8. Place the chicken onto grill grate and grill, covered for about 5–8 minutes per side.

9. Remove chicken from grill and cut into bite sized pieces.

10. In a large bowl, add the chicken pieces, strawberries, and spinach, and mix.

11. Place the reserved marinade and toss to coat. Serve immediately.

Nutrition:

Calories 356 Net Carbs 4 g Total Fat 21.4 g

Saturated Fat 4 g Cholesterol 101 mg

Sodium 143 mg Total Carbs 6.1 g

Fiber 2.1 g Sugar 3.8 g Protein 34.2 g

170. Tomato & Mozzarella Salad

Preparation time: 10 minutes

Cooking time: 0 minutes

Servings: 4

Ingredients:

- 4 cups cherry tomatoes, halved
- 1½ pounds mozzarella cheese, cubed
- ¼ cup fresh basil leaves, chopped
- ¼ cup olive oil
- 2 tablespoons fresh lemon juice
- 1 teaspoon fresh oregano, minced
- 1 teaspoon fresh parsley, minced
- 2–4 drops liquid stevia
- Salt and ground black pepper, as required

Directions:

1. In a salad bowl, mix together tomatoes, mozzarella, and basil.

2. In a small bowl, add remaining ingredients and beat until well combined.

3. Place dressing over salad and toss to coat well.

4. Serve immediately.

Nutrition:

Calories 87

Net Carbs 2.7 g

Total Fat 7.5 g

Saturated Fat 1.5 g

Cholesterol 3 mg

Sodium 57 mg

Total Carbs 3.9 g

Fiber 1.2 g

Sugar 2.5 g

Protein 2.4 g

171. Shrimp Salad

Preparation time: 15 minutes

Cooking time: 15 minutes

Servings: 6

Ingredients:

- 1 tablespoon unsalted butter
- 1 garlic clove, crushed and divided
- 2 tablespoons fresh rosemary, chopped
- 1 pound shrimp, peeled and deveined
- Salt and ground black pepper, as required
- 4 cups fresh arugula
- 2 cups lettuce, torn
- 2 tablespoons olive oil
- 2 tablespoons fresh lime juice

Directions:

1. In a large wok, melt the butter over medium heat and sauté 1 garlic clove for about 1 minute.

2. Add the shrimp with salt and black pepper and cook for about 4–5 minutes.

3. Remove from the heat and set aside to cool.

4. Ina large bowl, add the shrimp, arugula, oil, lime juice, salt, and black pepper, and gently toss to coat.

5. Serve immediately.

Nutrition:

Calories 157 Net Carbs 2.3 g

Total Fat 8.2 g Saturated Fat 2.4 g

Cholesterol 164 mg Sodium 230 mg

Total Carbs 3.1 g

Fiber 0.8 g

Sugar 0.5 g

Protein 17.7 g

172. Portobello Mushroom Pizza

Preparation Time: 15 minutes

Cooking Time: 5 minutes

Servings: 4

Ingredients:

- 4 large portobello mushrooms, stems removed
- ¼ cup olive oil
- 1 teaspoon minced garlic
- 1 medium tomato, cut into 4 slices
- 2 teaspoons chopped fresh basil
- 1 cup shredded mozzarella cheese

Directions:

1. Preheat the oven to broil. Line a baking sheet with aluminum foil and set aside.

2. In a small bowl, toss the mushroom caps with the olive oil until well coated. Use your fingertips to rub the oil in without breaking the mushrooms.

3. Place the mushrooms on the baking sheet gill-side down and broil the mushrooms until they are tender on the tops, about 2 minute

4. Flip the mushrooms over and broil 1 minute more

5. Take the baking sheet out and spread the garlic over each mushroom, top each with a tomato slice, sprinkle with the basil, and top with the cheese

6. Broil the mushrooms until the cheese is melted and bubbly, about 1 minute.

7. Serve.

Nutrition:

Calories: 251Fat: 20g

Protein: 14g

Carbs: 7g

Fiber: 3g

Net Carbs: 4g

Fat 71

Protein 19

Carbs 10

173. Garlicky Green Beans

Preparation Time: 10 minutes

Cooking Time: 10 minutes

Servings: 4

Ingredients:

- 1 pound green beans, stemmed
- 2 tablespoons olive oil

- 1 teaspoon minced garlic
- Sea salt
- Freshly ground black pepper
- ¼ cup freshly grated Parmesan cheese

Directions:

1. Preheat the oven to 425°F. Line a baking sheet with aluminum foil and set aside.
2. In a large bowl, toss together the green beans, olive oil, and garlic until well mixed.
3. Season the beans lightly with salt and pepper
4. Spread the beans on the baking sheet and roast them until they are tender and lightly browned, stirring them once, about 10 minutes.
5. Serve topped with the Parmesan cheese.

Nutrition:

Calories: 104 Fat: 9g

Protein: 4g Carbs: 2g

Fiber: 1g Net Carbs: 1g

Fat 77

Protein 15

Carbs 8

174. Sautéed Asparagus With Walnuts

Preparation Time: 10 minutes

Cooking Time: 5 minutes

Servings: 4

Ingredients:

- 1½ tablespoons olive oil
- ¾ pound asparagus, woody ends trimmed
- Sea salt
- Freshly ground pepper

- ¼ cup chopped walnuts

Directions:

1. Place a large skillet over medium-high heat and add the olive oil.
2. Sauté the asparagus until the spears are tender and lightly browned, about 5 minutes.
3. Season the asparagus with salt and pepper.
4. Remove the skillet from the heat and toss the asparagus with the walnuts.Serve.

Nutrition:

Calories: 124 Fat: 12g Protein: 3g

Carbs: 4g Fiber: 2g Net Carbs: 2g

Fat 81 Protein Carbs 10

175. Brussels Sprouts Casserole

Preparation Time: 15 minutes

Cooking Time: 30 minutes

Servings: 8

Ingredients:

- 8 bacon slices
- 1 pound Brussels sprouts, blanched for 10 minutes and cut into quarters

- 1 cup shredded Swiss cheese, divided
- ¾ cup heavy (whipping) cream

Directions:

1. Preheat the oven to 400°F.
2. Place a skillet over medium-high heat and cook the bacon until it is crispy, about 6 minutes.
3. Reserve 1 tablespoon of bacon fat to grease the casserole dish and roughly chop the cooked bacon.
4. Lightly oil a casserole dish with the reserved bacon fat and set aside.
5. In a medium bowl, toss the Brussels sprouts with the chopped bacon and ½ cup of cheese and transfer the mixture to the casserole dish.
6. Pour the heavy cream over the Brussels sprouts and top the casserole with the remaining ½ cup of cheese.
7. Bake until the cheese is melted and lightly browned and the vegetables are heated through, about 20 minutes.
8. Serve.

Nutrition:

Calories: 299

Fat: 11g

Protein: 12g

Carbs: 7g

Fiber: 3g

Net Carbs: 4g

Fat 77

Protein 15

Carbs 8

176. Creamed Spinach

Preparation Time: 10 minutes

Cooking Time: 30 minutes

Servings: 4

Ingredients:

- 1 tablespoon butter
- ½ sweet onion, very thinly sliced
- 4 cups spinach, stemmed and thoroughly washed
- ¾ cup heavy (whipping) cream
- ¼ cup Herbed Chicken Stock (here)
- Pinch sea salt
- Pinch freshly ground black pepper
- Pinch ground nutmeg

Directions:

1. In a large skillet over medium heat, add the butter.
2. Sauté the onion until it is lightly caramelized, about 5 minutes.
3. Stir in the spinach, heavy cream, chicken stock, salt, pepper, and nutmeg.
4. Sauté until the spinach is wilted, about 5 minutes.
5. Continue cooking the spinach until it is tender and the sauce is thickened, about 15 minutes.
6. Serve immediately.

Nutrition:

Calories: 195 Fat: 20g Protein: 3g

Carbs: 3g Fiber: 2g Net Carbs: 1g

Fat 88 Protein 6 Carbs 6

177. Cheesy Mashed Cauliflower

Preparation Time: 15 minutes

Cooking Time: 5 minutes

Servings: 4

Ingredients:

- 1 head cauliflower, chopped roughly
- ½ cup shredded Cheddar cheese
- ¼ cup heavy (whipping) cream
- 2 tablespoons butter, at room temperature
- Sea salt
- Freshly ground black pepper

Directions:

1. Place a large saucepan filled three-quarters full with water over high heat and bring to a boil.
2. Blanch the cauliflower until tender, about 5 minutes, and drain.
3. Transfer the cauliflower to a food processor and add the cheese, heavy cream, and butter. Purée until very creamy and whipped.
4. Season with salt and pepper.
5. Serve.

Nutrition:

Calories: 183

Fat: 15g

Protein: 8g

Carbs: 6g

Fiber: 2g

Net Carbs: 4g

Fat 75

Protein 14

Carbs 11

178. Sautéed Crispy Zucchini

Preparation Time: 15 minutes

Cooking Time: 10 minutes

Servings: 4

Ingredients:

- 2 tablespoons butter
- 4 zucchini, cut into ¼-inch-thick rounds
- ½ cup freshly grated Parmesan cheese
- Freshly ground black pepper

Directions:

1. Place a large skillet over medium-high heat and melt the butter.

2. Add the zucchini and sauté until tender and lightly browned, about 5 minutes.

3. Spread the zucchini evenly in the skillet and sprinkle the Parmesan cheese over the vegetables.

4. Cook without stirring until the Parmesan cheese is melted and crispy where it touches the skillet, about 5 minutes.

5. Serve.

Nutrition:

Calories: 94

Fat: 8g

Protein: 4g

Carbs: 1g

Fiber: 0g

Net Carbs: 1g

Fat 76

Protein 20

Carbs 4

179. Mushrooms With Camembert

Preparation Time: 5 minutes

Cooking Time: 15 minutes

Servings: 4

Ingredients:

- 2 tablespoons butter
- 2 teaspoons minced garlic
- 1 pound button mushrooms, halved
- 4 ounces Camembert cheese, diced
- Freshly ground black pepper

Directions:

1. Place a large skillet over medium-high heat and melt the butter.

2. Sauté the garlic until translucent, about 3 minutes.

3. Sauté the mushrooms until tender, about 10 minutes.

4. Stir in the cheese and sauté until melted, about 2 minutes.

5. Season with pepper and serve.

Nutrition:

Calories: 161 Fat: 13g

Protein: 9g Carbs: 4g

Fiber: 1g

Net Carbs: 3g

Fat 70

Protein 21

Carbs 9

180. Pesto Zucchini Noodles

Preparation Time: 15 minutes

Cooking Time: 10 minutes

Servings: 4

Ingredients:

- 4 small zucchini, ends trimmed
- ¾ cup Herb Kale Pesto (here) ¼ cup grated or shredded
- Parmesan chees

Directions:

1. Use a spiralizer or peeler to cut the zucchini into "noodles" and place them in a medium bowl.

2. Add the pesto and the Parmesan cheese and toss to coat.

3. Serve.

Nutrition:

Calories: 93 Fat: 8g

Protein: 4g Carbs: 2g

Fiber: 0g Net Carbs: 2g Fat 70

Protein 15 Carbs 8

181.   Golden Rosti

Preparation Time: 15 minutes

Cooking Time: 15 minutes

Servings: 8

Ingredients:

- 8 bacon slices, chopped
- 1 cup shredded acorn squash
- 1 cup shredded raw celeriac
- 2 tablespoons grated or shredded Parmesan cheese
- 2 teaspoons minced garlic
- 1 teaspoon chopped fresh thyme
- Sea salt
- Freshly ground black pepper
- 2 tablespoons butter

Directions:

1. In a large skillet over medium-high heat, cook the bacon until crispy, about 5 minutes.
2. While the bacon is cooking, mix together the squash, celeriac, Parmesan cheese, garlic, and thyme in a large bowl. Season the mixture generously with salt and pepper, and set aside.
3. Remove the cooked bacon with a slotted spoon to the rosti mixture and stir to incorporate.
4. Remove all but 2 tablespoons of bacon fat from the skillet and add the butter

5. Reduce the heat to medium-low and transfer the rosti mixture to the skillet and spread it out evenly to form a large round patty about 1 inch thick.
6. Cook until the bottom of the rosti is golden brown and crisp, about 5 minutes.
7. Flip the rosti over and cook until the other side is crispy and the middle is cooked through, about 5 minutes more.
8. Remove the skillet from the heat and cut the rosti into 8 pieces
9. Serve.

Nutrition:

Calories: 171Fat: 15g Protein: 5g

Carbs: 3g Fiber: 0g Net Carbs: 3g

Fat 81Protein 12 Carbs 7

182.   Artichoke and Avocado Pasta Salad

Preparation Time: 15 minutes

Cooking Time: 30 minutes

Servings: 10 servings

Ingredients:

- Two cups of spiral pasta (uncooked)
- A quarter cup of Romano cheese (grated)
- One can (fourteen oz.) of artichoke hearts (coarsely chopped and drained well)
- One avocado (medium-sized, ripe, cubed)

- Two plum tomatoes (chopped coarsely)

For the dressing:

- One tablespoon. of fresh cilantro (chopped)
- Two tablespoons. of lime juice
- A quarter cup of canola oil
- One and a half teaspoons. of lime zest (grated)
- Half a teaspoon. each of
- Pepper (freshly ground)
- Kosher salt

Directions:

1. Follow the directions mentioned on the package for cooking the pasta. Drain them well and rinse using cold water.
2. Then, take a large-sized bowl and in it, add the pasta along with the tomatoes, artichoke hearts, cheese, and avocado. Combine them well. Then, take another bowl and add all the ingredients of the dressing in it. Whisk them together and, once combined, add the dressing over the pasta.
3. Gently toss the mixture to coat everything evenly in the dressing and then refrigerate.

Nutrition:

Calories: 188 Protein: 6g Fat: 10g
Carbs: 21g Fiber: 2g

183. Apple Arugula and Turkey Salad in a Jar

Preparation Time: 10 minutes
Cooking Time: 10 minutes
Servings: 4 servings
Ingredients:

- Three tablespoons. of red wine vinegar
- Two tablespoons. of chives (freshly minced)
- Half a cup of orange juice
- One to three tablespoons. of sesame oil
- A quarter teaspoon. each of
- Pepper (coarsely ground)
- Salt

For the salad:

- Four teaspoons. of curry powder
- Four cups each of
- Turkey (cubed, cooked)
- Baby spinach or fresh arugula
- A quarter teaspoon. of salt
- Half a teaspoon. of pepper (coarsely ground)
- One cup of halved green grapes
- One apple (large-sized, chopped)
- Eleven oz. of mandarin oranges (properly drained)
- One tablespoon. of lemon juice
- Half a cup each of
- Walnuts (chopped)
- Dried cranberries or pomegranate seeds

Directions:

1. Take a small-sized bowl and add the first 6 ingredients from the list into it. Whisk them. Then take a large bowl and add the turkey and then add the seasonings on top of it. Toss the turkey cubes to coat them with the seasoning. Take another bowl and add the lemon juice and toss the apple chunks in the juice.
2. Take four jars and divide the layers in the order I mention here - first goes the orange juice mixture, the second layer is that of the turkey, then apple, oranges, grapes, cranberries or pomegranate seeds,

walnuts, and spinach or arugula. Cover the jars and then refrigerate them.

Nutrition:

Calories: 471

Protein: 45g

Fat: 19g

Carbs: 33g

Fiber: 5g

184.   Summertime Slaw

Preparation Time: 20 minutes

Cooking Time: 30 minutes

Servings: 10-12 servings

Ingredients:

- One-third cup of canola oil
- Three-quarter cups each of
- White vinegar
- Sugar
- One teaspoon. each of
- Pepper
- Salt
- One tablespoon. of water
- Half a teaspoon. of red pepper flakes (crushed and optional)
- Two tomatoes (medium-sized, seeded, peeled, and chopped)
- One pack of coleslaw mix (fourteen oz.)
- One sweet red pepper (small-sized, chopped)
- One green pepper (small-sized, chopped)
- One onion (large-sized, chopped)
- Half a cup of sweet pickle relish

Directions:

1. Take a saucepan of large size and in it, combine water, sugar, oil, vinegar,

pepper, salt, and if you want, then red pepper flakes too. Cook them over medium heat by continuously stirring the mixture. Keep stirring until it comes to a boil. Cook for another two minutes or so and make sure that all the sugar has dissolved. Once done, cool the mixture to room temperature by stirring it.

2. Take a salad bowl of large size and in it, combine the pickle relish, coleslaw mix, peppers, onion, and tomatoes. On top of the mixture, add the dressing and toss the mixture to coat it properly. Cover the mixture and put it in the refrigerator for a night.

Nutrition:

Calories: 138

Protein: 1g Fat: 6g

Carbs: 21g

Fiber: 2g

185.   Zucchini and Tomato Spaghetti

Preparation Time: 10 minutes

Cooking Time: 20 minutes

Servings: 4 servings

Ingredients:

- Two large-sized zucchini nicely spiralized
- Three cups of red and yellow cherry tomatoes
- Four oz. of spaghetti (whole wheat – optional)
- Toppings – grated parmesan

For the avocado sauce:

- A quarter cup of olive oil
- One avocado
- Half a cup of parsley (fresh)
- Half a teaspoon. of salt

- Three-four green onions (only the green parts)
- One lemon (juiced)
- One clove of garlic
- A pinch of pepper (freshly ground)

Directions:

1. Firstly, take all the sauce ingredients and pulse them so that they are combined well and form a smooth mixture. Set it aside.

2. Then, follow the directions mentioned in the package for cooking the spaghetti. Drain the cooked spaghetti and keep it aside too.

3. Take a large-sized skillet and heat the cherry tomatoes in it. Use a bit of olive oil. Keep cooking the tomatoes until they seem well-roasted, and they will also seem loosened with their skins split. Once done, remove the tomatoes from the flame and set it aside.

4. Then, add the zucchini to the same skillet. Stir and toss them for about two minutes until they look crisp. Then, add the avocado sauce and the spaghetti. Keep tossing until everything has properly combined. Season with pepper and salt as per taste. Top with parmesan and the tomatoes that you had reserved earlier.

Nutrition:

Calories: 330 Protein: 7.1g

Fat: 20g Carbs: 35.3g Fiber: 8g

186.   White Bean Salad

Preparation Time: 5 minutes

Cooking Time: 10 minutes

Servings: 4 servings

Ingredients:

For the salad:

- Two green peppers coarsely chopped
- Half a cup each of
- Chopped cucumber
- Chopped tomatoes
- One and a half cups of white beans (boiled)
- A quarter cup each of
- Green onions (chopped)
- Fresh dill (chopped)
- Parsley (chopped)
- Four eggs (hard-boiled)

For the dressing:

- One tablespoon. of lemon juice
- One teaspoon. of vinegar
- Two tablespoons. of olive oil
- One teaspoon. of sumac
- Half a teaspoon. of salt
- For quick onion pickle,
- One teaspoon. each of

- Sumac

- Salt

- Vinegar

- One tablespoon. of lemon juice

- Two thinly sliced red onions (medium-sized)

- Two cups of water (hot)

Directions:

1. Take a large-sized bowl and add all the salad ingredients in it, but keep the eggs aside.

2. In case you do not want to pickle the onions, you can simply make thin slices and then mix them with the other ingredients. But, if you do want to pickle the onions, then continue with it before you move on to the dressing. The recipe for the onions is mentioned later.

3. Take all the ingredients of the dressing together in one bowl and whisk them together. Then, drizzle the dressing over the salad. Toss well, and on the top, place halved eggs.

For the pickled onions:

1. First, take very hot water and place the sliced onions in it. Blanch the onions for one minute and then immediately transfer them into a pot of very cold water so that the cooking stops. Let them stay in that pot of cold water for a few minutes. Once done, drain them well.

2. Mix sumac, lemon juice, salt, and vinegar together and then pour the mixture over the onion that you just drained. Keep it for five to ten minutes.

3. Then, add the onions into the mixture of salad and stir well. Keep some onions aside so that you can use them as a topping.

Nutrition:

Calories: 449

Protein: 23.6g

Fat: 23.3g

Carbs: 39.7g

187.   Lentil Bolognese

Preparation Time: 20 minutes

Cooking Time: 40 minutes

Servings: 4-6 servings

Ingredients:

- Two boxes of penne pasta

- One onion (medium-sized, finely chopped)

- One red bell pepper (finely chopped)

- Two tablespoons. of olive oil

- Two carrots (large-sized, sliced)

- Four cloves of garlic (large ones, minced)

- One tablespoon. of miso

- One teaspoon. each of

- Pepper

- Salt

- Four cups of water

- One can of tomato paste (measuring five and a half ounces)

- One cup each of

- Brown lentils (dried)

- Cherry tomatoes (halved)

- Toppings (optional) – black pepper, sage leaves, parmesan (grated)

Directions:

1. Take a large-sized skillet and start by heating the oil in it on medium flame. Then, add the chopped onions. In about five minutes, they will soften and appear to be translucent. Then, add the red

pepper, carrots, sugar, and sea salt to the skillet and keep cooking. Stir the mixture from time to time. In fifteen minutes, everything will be well caramelized. Then, add the tomato paste and the garlic and let the mixture cook for three minutes or until you get a caramelized fragrance from the paste.

2. Then, add the lentils, miso, and water to the skillet and bring the mixture to a boil. Once the mixture is boiling, reduce the flame and keep the skillet uncovered while the lentils are cooking. This will take about twenty-five to thirty minutes. Keep stirring the lentils from time to time, and in case they look dry, add some water. After that, add the cherry tomatoes and keep stirring.

3. While you are cooking the lentils, take a large pot and fill it with water. Add generous amounts of salt and bring the water to a boil. Then, add the chickpea pasta into the water and cook it for about five to six minutes or until al dente. Don't overcook it. Once done, drain the water and set them aside to cool.

4. Divide the penne into four to six meal prep containers and top with Bolognese. Sprinkle a few sage leaves or a bit of parmesan if you want.

Nutrition:

Calories: 486 Protein: 29.3g

Fat: 9g Carbs: 78.2g Fiber: 15g

188. Kale, Lemon, and White Bean Soup

Preparation Time: 20 minutes

Cooking Time: 1 hour 10 minutes

Servings: 2 servings

Ingredients:

- One hundred fifty grams of dried cannellini beans
- Two cups of vegetable stock
- Five cups of water
- One white onion (large-sized, diced)
- Two tablespoons. of olive oil
- Eight cloves of garlic
- Kombu (one-inch strip)
- One teaspoon. of dried thyme
- Two potatoes (small ones, cubed after peeling)
- Two bay leaves
- One cup of kale
- One lemon (juiced and zest)

Directions:

1. Take an ample amount of water to soak the dried beans and keep them soaked for about twelve hours. Drain the beans properly and they should become double their size. Rinse them and they are ready to be cooked.

2. Take a large-sized pot, and in it, add one tablespoon. of oil and heat it. Then, add the diced onion in the pot and cook the onions until they become golden and soft.

3. Then, add the stock and water and garlic, dried beans, kombu, thyme, and bay leaves. Keep the pot covered and then bring it to a boil. Once it starts boiling, reduce the flame to a simmer and wait for about forty minutes.

4. While it is cooking, start with the kale. Wash it thoroughly. All the tough inner stalks should be removed. Then, start slicing them into ribbons of one-inch each. It looks good when you have delicate

small pieces, so you should take your time with this.

5. After about half an hour, add the potatoes to the pot and then let the preparation simmer for ten more minutes. After this, both the potatoes and the beans should be soft. Take out the kombu and bay leaves. Take a potato masher and use it carefully to mash at least half of the beans and potatoes.

6. Add the kale. Cook the mixture for ten more minutes. The water content needs to be checked now and see whether it is right or whether it needs to be topped up. If the water is too much, then cook uncovered for a few minutes to dries up.

7. Once you notice the kale softening, take a tablespoon. of olive oil and add it to the pot. Stir in the zest and lemon juice as well, and your dish is ready.

Nutrition:

Calories: 574 Protein: 22g

 Fat: 16g

Carbs: 106g Fiber: 23g

189. Aloo Gobi

Preparation Time: 15 Minutes

Cooking Time: 4 To 5 Hours

Servings: 4

Ingredients:

- 1 large cauliflower, cut into 1-inch pieces
- 1 large russet potato, peeled and diced
- 1 medium yellow onion, peeled and diced
- 1 cup canned diced tomatoes, with juice
- 1 cup frozen peas
- ¼ cup water
- 1 (2-inch) piece fresh ginger, peeled and finely chopped
- 1½ teaspoons minced garlic (3 cloves)
- 1 jalapeño pepper, stemmed and sliced
- 1 tablespoon cumin seeds
- 1 tablespoon garam masala
- 1 teaspoon ground turmeric
- 1 heaping tablespoon fresh cilantro
- Cooked rice, for serving (optional)

Directions:

1. Combine the cauliflower, potato, onion, diced tomatoes, peas, water, ginger, garlic, jalapeño, cumin seeds, garam masala, and turmeric in a slow cooker; mix until well combined.

2. Cover and cook on low for 4 to 5 hours.

3. Garnish with the cilantro, and serve over cooked rice (if using).

Nutrition:

Calories: 115

Total fat: 1g

Protein: 6g

Sodium: 62mg

Fiber: 6g

190.   Jackfruit Carnitas

Preparation Time: 15 Minutes

Cooking Time: 8 Hours

Servings: 4

Ingredients:

- 2 (20-ounce) cans jackfruit, drained, hard pieces discarded
- ¾ cup Very Easy Vegetable Broth (here) or store bought
- 1 tablespoon ground cumin
- 1 tablespoon dried oregano
- 1½ teaspoons ground coriander
- 1 teaspoon minced garlic (2 cloves)
- ½ teaspoon ground cinnamon
- 2 bay leaves
- Tortillas, for serving
- Optional toppings: diced onions, sliced radishes, fresh cilantro, lime wedges, Nacho Cheese (here)

Directions:

1. Combine the jackfruit, vegetable broth, cumin, oregano, coriander, garlic, cinnamon, and bay leaves in a slow cooker. Stir to combine.
2. Cover and cook on low for 8 hours or on high for 4 hours.
3. Use two forks to pull the jackfruit apart into shreds.
4. Remove the bay leaves. Serve in warmed tortillas with your favorite taco fixings.

Nutrition:

Calories: 286 Total fat: 2g

Protein: 6g Sodium: 155mg Fiber: 5g

191.   Baked Beans

Preparation Time: 15 Minutes

Cooking Time: 6 Hours

Servings: 4

Ingredients:

- 2 (15-ounce) cans white beans, drained and rinsed
- 1 (15-ounce) can tomato sauce
- 1 medium yellow onion, finely diced
- 1½ teaspoons minced garlic (3 cloves)
- 3 tablespoons brown sugar
- 2 tablespoons molasses
- 1 tablespoon prepared yellow mustard
- 1 tablespoon chili powder
- 1 teaspoon soy sauce
- Pinch salt
- Freshly ground black pepper

Directions:

1. Place the beans, tomato sauce, onion, garlic, brown sugar, molasses, mustard, chili powder, and soy sauce into a slow cooker; mix well.
2. Cover and cook on low for 6 hours. Season with salt and pepper before serving.

Nutrition:

Calories: 468

Total fat: 2g

Protein: 28g

Sodium: 714mg

Fiber: 20g

192. Brussels Sprouts Curry

Preparation Time: 15 Minutes

Cooking Time: 7 To 8 Hours

Servings: 4

Ingredients:

- ¾ pound Brussels sprouts, bottoms cut off and sliced in half
- 1 can full-fat coconut milk
- 1 cup Very Easy Vegetable Broth (here) or store bought
- 1 medium onion, diced
- 1 medium carrot, thinly sliced
- 1 medium red or Yukon potato, diced
- 1½ teaspoons minced garlic (3 cloves)
- 1 (1-inch) piece fresh ginger, peeled and minced
- 1 small serrano chile, seeded and finely chopped
- 2 tablespoons peanut butter
- 1 tablespoon rice vinegar or other vinegar
- 1 tablespoon cane sugar or agave nectar
- 1 tablespoon soy sauce
- 1 teaspoon curry powder
- 1 teaspoon ground turmeric
- Pinch salt
- Freshly ground black pepper
- Cooked rice, for serving (optional)

Directions:

Place the Brussels sprouts, coconut milk, vegetable broth, onion, carrot, potato, garlic, ginger, serrano chile, peanut butter, vinegar, cane sugar, soy sauce, curry powder, and turmeric in a slow cooker. Mix well.

Cover and cook on low for 7 to 8 hours or on high for 4 to 5 hours.

Season with salt and pepper. Serve over rice (if using).

Nutrition:

Calories: 404

Total fat: 29g

Protein: 10g

Sodium: 544mg

Fiber: 8g

193. Jambalaya

Preparation Time: 15 Minutes

Cooking Time: 6 To 8 Hours

Servings: 4

Ingredients:

- 2 cups Very Easy Vegetable Broth (here) or store bought
- 1 large yellow onion, diced
- 1 green bell pepper, seeded and chopped
- 2 celery stalks, chopped
- 1½ teaspoons minced garlic (3 cloves)

- 1 (15-ounce) can dark red kidney beans, drained and rinsed

- 1 (15-ounce) can black-eyed peas, drained and rinsed

- 1 (15-ounce) can diced tomatoes, drained

- 2 tablespoons Cajun seasoning

- 2 teaspoons dried oregano

- 2 teaspoons dried parsley

- 1 teaspoon cayenne pepper

- 1 teaspoon smoked paprika

- ½ teaspoon dried thyme

- Cooked rice, for serving (optional)

Directions:

1. Combine the vegetable broth, onion, bell pepper, celery, garlic, kidney beans, black-eyed peas, diced tomatoes, Cajun seasoning, oregano, parsley, cayenne pepper, smoked paprika, and dried thyme in a slow cooker; mix well.

2. Cover and cook on low for 6 to 8 hours.

3. Serve over rice (if using).

Nutrition:

Calories: 428 Total fat: 2g

Protein: 28g Sodium: 484mg Fiber: 19g

194. Mushroom-Kale Stroganoff

Preparation Time: 15 Minutes

Cooking Time: 6 To 8 Hours

Servings: 4

Ingredients:

- 1 pound mushrooms, sliced

- 1½ cups Very Easy Vegetable Broth (here) or store bought

- 1 cup stemmed and chopped kale

- 1 small yellow onion, diced

- 2 garlic cloves, minced

- 2 tablespoons all-purpose flour

- 2 tablespoons ketchup or tomato paste

- 2 teaspoons paprika

- ½ cup vegan sour cream

- ¼ cup chopped fresh parsley

- Cooked rice, pasta, or quinoa, for serving

Directions:

4. Combine the mushrooms, vegetable broth, kale, onion, garlic, flour, ketchup or tomato paste, and paprika in a slow cooker. Mix thoroughly.

5. Cover and cook on low for 6 to 8 hours.

6. Stir in the sour cream and parsley just before serving.

7. Serve over rice, pasta, or quinoa.

Nutrition:

Calories: 146 Total fat: 7g

Protein: 8g Sodium: 417mg Fiber: 3g

195. Sloppy Joe Filling

Preparation Time: 15 Minutes

Cooking Time: 6 To 8 Hours

Servings: 4

Ingredients:

- 3 cups textured vegetable protein

- 3 cups water

- 2 (6-ounce) cans tomato paste, or 1 cup ketchup

- 1 medium yellow onion, diced

- ½ medium green bell pepper, finely diced

- 2 teaspoons minced garlic (4 cloves)
- 4 tablespoons vegan Worcestershire sauce
- 3 tablespoons brown sugar
- 3 tablespoons apple cider vinegar
- 3 tablespoons prepared yellow mustard
- 2 tablespoons hot sauce (optional)
- 1 tablespoon salt
- 1 teaspoon chili powder
- Sliced, toasted buns or cooked rice, for serving

Directions:

1. Combine the textured vegetable protein, water, tomato paste, onion, bell pepper, garlic, Worcestershire sauce, brown sugar, vinegar, mustard, hot sauce (if using), salt, and chili powder in a slow cooker. Mix well.
2. Cover and cook on low for 6 to 8 hours or on high for 4 to 5 hours.
3. Serve on sliced, toasted buns or over rice.

Nutrition:

Calories: 452 Total fat: 4g

Protein: 75g Sodium: 2,242mg

Fiber: 11g

196.   Hoppin' John

Preparation Time: 15 Minutes

Cooking Time: 4 To 6 Hours

Servings: 4

Ingredients:

- 3 (15-ounce) cans black-eyed peas, drained and rinsed
- 1 (14.5-ounce) can Cajun-style stewed tomatoes, with juice
- 2 cups hot water
- 1 cup stemmed and chopped kale
- ¾ cup finely diced red bell pepper
- ½ cup sliced scallions
- 1 medium jalapeño pepper, seeded and minced
- 1 teaspoon minced garlic (2 cloves)
- 1½ teaspoons hot sauce
- 1 vegetable bouillon cube
- Cooked rice, for serving

Directions:

1. Combine the black-eyed peas, tomatoes, hot water, kale, bell pepper, scallions, jalapeño, garlic, hot sauce, and bouillon cube in a slow cooker. Stir to combine.
2. Cover and cook on low for 4 to 6 hours.
3. Serve over cooked rice.

Nutrition:

Calories: 164

Total fat: 2g

Protein: 10g

Sodium: 250mg

Fiber: 8g

197. African Sweet Potato Stew

Preparation time: 15 minutes

Cooking time: 7 to 8 hours

Servings: 4

Ingredients:

- 4 cups peeled diced sweet potatoes
- 1 (15-ounce) can red kidney beans, drained and rinsed
- 1 (14.5-ounce) can diced tomatoes, drained
- 1 cup diced red bell pepper
- 2 cups Very Easy Vegetable Broth (here) or store bought
- 1 medium yellow onion, chopped
- 1 (4.5-ounce) can chopped green chiles, drained
- 1 teaspoon minced garlic (2 cloves)
- 1½ teaspoons ground ginger
- 1 teaspoon ground cumin
- 4 tablespoons creamy peanut butter
- Pinch salt
- Freshly ground black pepper

Directions:

1. Combine the sweet potatoes, kidney beans, diced tomatoes, bell pepper, vegetable broth, onion, green chiles, garlic, ginger, and cumin in a slow cooker. Mix well
2. Cover and cook on low for 7 to 8 hours.
3. Ladle a little of the soup into a small bowl and mix in the peanut butter, then pour the mixture back into the stew
4. Season with salt and pepper. Mix well and serve.

Nutrition:

Calories: 514 Total fat: 10g

Protein: 22g Sodium: 649mg

Fiber: 17g

198. Sweet-And-Sour Tempeh

Preparation Time: 15 Minutes

Cooking Time: 7 To 8 Hours

Servings: 4

Ingredients:

For The Sauce:

- ¾ cup fresh or canned pineapple chunks
- ½ cup crushed tomatoes
- ½ cup water
- ¼ cup chopped onion
- ¼ cup soy sauce
- 2 tablespoons rice vinegar
- ¼ teaspoon red pepper flakes
- 1 (½-inch) piece fresh ginger, peeled

For The Tempeh:

- 2 (8-ounce) packages tempeh, cut into cubes
- 2 cups diced bell pepper

- 1½ cups diced pineapple

- ½ cup diced onion

- Cooked rice, for serving

Directions:

1. Put the pineapple chunks, crushed tomatoes, water, onion, soy sauce, rice vinegar, red pepper flakes, and ginger in a blender; blend until smooth.

2. Combine the sauce, tempeh, bell pepper, diced pineapple, and onion in a slow cooker; stir well.

3. Cover and cook on low for 7 to 8 hours.

4. Serve over cooked rice.

Nutrition:

Calories: 324 Total fat: 13g Protein: 24g

Sodium: 974mg Fiber: 4g

199. Jackfruit Cochinita Pibil

Preparation Time: 15 Minutes

Cooking Time: 8 Hours

Servings: 4

Ingredients:

- 2 (20-ounce) cans jackfruit, drained, hard pieces discarded

- 2/3 cup freshly squeezed lemon juice

- 1/3 cup orange juice

- 2 habanero peppers, seeded and chopped

- 2 tablespoons achiote paste

- 2 teaspoons ground cumin

- 2 teaspoons smoked paprika

- 2 teaspoons chili powder

- 2 teaspoons ground coriander

- Pinch salt

- Freshly ground black pepper

- Warmed corn tortillas, for serving

Directions:

1. Combine the jackfruit, lemon juice, orange juice, habanero peppers, achiote paste, cumin, smoked paprika, chili powder, and coriander in a slow cooker; mix well.

2. Cover and cook on low for 8 hours or on high for 4 hours.

3. Use two forks to pull the jackfruit apart into shreds. Season with salt and pepper.

4. Heat tortillas directly over a gas fire, or in a skillet over medium heat for about 1 minute per side. Spoon the jackfruit into the tortillas and serve.

Nutrition:

Calories: 297 Total fat: 2g

Protein: 5g Sodium: 71mg Fiber: 6g

200. Delightful Dal

Preparation Time: 15 Minutes

Cooking Time: 7 To 9 Hours

Servings: 4

Ingredients:

- 3 cups red lentils, rinsed

- 6 cups water

- 1 (28-ounce) can diced tomatoes, with juice

- 1 small yellow onion, diced

- 2½ teaspoons minced garlic (5 cloves)

- 1 (1-inch) piece fresh ginger, peeled and minced
- 1 tablespoon ground turmeric
- 2 teaspoons ground cumin
- 1½ teaspoons ground cardamom
- 1½ teaspoons whole mustard seeds
- 1 teaspoon fennel seeds
- 1 bay leaf
- 1 teaspoon salt
- ¼ teaspoon freshly ground black pepper

Directions:

1. Combine the lentils, water, diced tomatoes, onion, garlic, ginger, turmeric, cumin, cardamom, mustard seeds, fennel seeds, bay leaf, salt, and pepper in a slow cooker; mix well.
2. Cover and cook on low for 7 to 9 hours or on high for 4 to 6 hours.
3. Remove the bay leaf, and serve.

Nutrition:

Calories: 585 Total fat: 4g Protein: 40g

Sodium: 616mg Fiber: 48g

201.   Moroccan Chickpea Stew

Preparation Time: 15 Minutes

Cooking Time: 6 To 8 Hours

Servings: 4

Ingredients:

- 1 small butternut squash, peeled and chopped into bite-size pieces
- 3 cups Very Easy Vegetable Broth (here) or store bought
- 1 medium yellow onion, diced
- 1 bell pepper, diced
- 1 (15-ounce) can chickpeas, drained and rinsed
- 1 (14.5-ounce) can tomato sauce
- ¾ cup brown lentils, rinsed
- 1½ teaspoons minced garlic (3 cloves)
- 1½ teaspoons ground ginger
- 1½ teaspoons ground turmeric
- 1½ teaspoons ground cumin
- 1 teaspoon ground cinnamon
- ¾ teaspoon smoked paprika
- ½ teaspoon salt
- 1 (8-ounce) package fresh udon noodles
- Freshly ground black pepper

Directions:

1. Combine the butternut squash, vegetable broth, onion, bell pepper, chickpeas, tomato sauce, brown lentils, garlic, ginger, turmeric, cumin, cinnamon, smoked paprika, and salt in a slow cooker. Mix well.
2. Cover and cook 6 to 8 hours on low or 3 to 4 hours on high. In the last 10 minutes of cooking, add the noodles.
3. Season with pepper, and serve.

Nutrition: Calories: 427 Total fat: 4g

Protein: 26g Sodium: 1,423mg Fiber: 24g

CHAPTER 9:

60 Days Meal Plan

Day	Breakfast	Lunch	Dinner
1	Cheese Crepes	Easy Keto Smoked Salmon Lunch Bowl.	Green Chicken Curry
2	Ricotta Pancakes	Easy One-Pan Ground Beef And Green Beans	Creamy Pork Stew
3	Yogurt Waffles	Easy Spinach And Bacon Salad	Salmon & Shrimp Stew
4	Broccoli Muffins	Easy Keto Italian Plate	Chicken Casserole
5	Pumpkin Bread	Fresh Broccoli And Dill Keto Salad	Creamy Chicken Bake
6	Eggs in Avocado Cups	Keto Smoked Salmon Filled Avocados.	Beef & Veggie Casserole
7	Cheddar Scramble	Low-Carb Broccoli Lemon Parmesan Soup	Beef with Bell Peppers
8	Bacon Omelet	Prosciutto And Mozzarella Bomb	Braised Lamb shanks
9	Green Veggies Quiche	Summer Tuna Avocado Salad	Shrimp & Bell Pepper Stir-Fry
10	Chicken & Asparagus Frittata	Mushrooms & Goat Cheese Salad	Veggies & Walnut Loaf
11	Southwest Scrambled Egg Bites	Keto Bacon Sushi	Keto Sloppy Joes
12	Bacon Egg Bites	Cole Slaw Keto Wrap	Low Carb Crack Slaw Egg Roll in a Bowl Recipe
13	Omelet Bites	Keto Chicken Club Lettuce Wrap	Low Carb Beef Stir Fry
14	Cheddar & Bacon Egg Bites	Keto Broccoli Salad	One Pan Pesto Chicken and Veggies
15	Avocado Pico Egg Bites	Keto Sheet Pan Chicken and Rainbow Veggies	Crispy Peanut Tofu and Cauliflower Rice Stir-Fry
16	Salmon Scramble	Skinny Bang-Bang Zucchini Noodles	Simple Keto Fried Chicken

17	Mexican Scrambled Eggs	Keto Caesar Salad	Keto Butter Chicken
18	Caprese Omelet	Keto Buffalo Chicken Empanadas	Keto Shrimp Scampi Recipe
19	Sausage Omelet	Pepperoni and Cheddar Stromboli	Keto Lasagna
20	Brown Hash with Zucchini	Tuna Casserole	Creamy Tuscan Garlic Chicken
21	Cheese Crepes	Brussels Sprout and Hamburger Gratin	Ancho Macho Chili
22	Ricotta Pancakes	Carpaccio	Chicken Supreme Pizza
23	Yogurt Waffles	Keto Croque Monsieur	Baked Jerked Chicken
24	Broccoli Muffins	Keto Wraps With Cream Cheese And Salmon	Chicken Schnitzel
25	Pumpkin Bread	Savory Keto Broccoli Cheese Muffins	Broccoli and Chicken Casserole
26	Eggs in Avocado Cups	Keto Rusk	Baked Fish with Lemon Butter
27	Cheddar Scramble	Flaxseed Hemp Flour Bun	Chicken Broccoli Alfredo
28	Bacon Omelet	Keto Muffins With Roquefort	Grilled Cheesy Buffalo Chicken
29	Green Veggies Quiche	Keto Wrap	Middle Eastern Shawarma.
30	Chicken & Asparagus Frittata	Savory Keto Muffins	Tex Mex Casserole
31	Southwest Scrambled Egg Bites	Turkey and Cream Cheese Sauce	Dinner
32	Bacon Egg Bites	Baked Salmon and Pesto	Spicy Steak Curry
33	Omelet Bites	Keto Chicken with Butter and Lemon	Beef Stew
34	Cheddar & Bacon Egg Bites	Garlic Chicken	Beef & Cabbage Stew
35	Avocado Pico Egg Bites	Salmon Skewers Wrapped with Prosciutto	Beef & Mushroom Chili
36	Salmon Scramble	Buffalo Drumsticks and Chili Aioli	Steak with Cheese Sauce

37		Mexican Scrambled Eggs	Slow Cooked Roasted Pork and Creamy Gravy	Steak with Blueberry Sauce
38		Caprese Omelet	Bacon-Wrapped Meatloaf	Grilled Steak
39		Sausage Omelet	Lamb Chops and Herb Butter	Roasted Tenderloin
40		Brown Hash with Zucchini	Crispy Cuban Pork Roast	Garlicky Prime Rib Roast
41		Cheese Crepes	Keto Barbecued Ribs	Beef Taco Bake
42		Ricotta Pancakes	Turkey Burgers and Tomato Butter	Chocolate Chili
43		Yogurt Waffles	Keto Hamburger	Pork Stew
44		Broccoli Muffins	Chicken Wings and Blue Cheese Dressing	Pork & Chiles Stew
45		Pumpkin Bread	Salmon Burgers with Lemon Butter and Mash	Dinner
46		Eggs in Avocado Cups	Egg salad recipe	Baked Fish Fillets with Vegetables in Foil
47		Cheddar Scramble	Taco Stuffed Avocados	Fish & Chips
48		Bacon Omelet	Buffalo Shrimp Lettuce Wraps	Baked Salmon with Almonds and Cream Sauce
49		Green Veggies Quiche	Broccoli Bacon Salad	Shrimp and Sausage Bake
50		Chicken & Asparagus Frittata	Keto Egg Salad	Herb Butter Scallops
51		Cheese Crepes		Pan-Seared Halibut with Citrus Butter Sauce
52		Ricotta Pancakes	Baked Salmon and Pesto	Baked Coconut Haddock
53		Yogurt Waffles	Keto Chicken with Butter and Lemon	Green Chicken Curry
54		Broccoli Muffins	Garlic Chicken	Creamy Pork Stew
55		Pumpkin Bread	Salmon Skewers Wrapped with Prosciutto	Salmon & Shrimp Stew
56		Eggs in Avocado Cups	Buffalo Drumsticks and Chili Aioli	Chicken Casserole
57		Cheddar Scramble	Slow Cooked Roasted Pork and Creamy Gravy	Creamy Chicken Bake

58	Bacon Omelet	Bacon-Wrapped Meatloaf	Beef & Veggie Casserole
59	Green Veggies Quiche	Lamb Chops and Herb Butter	Beef with Bell Peppers
60	Chicken & Asparagus Frittata	Crispy Cuban Pork Roast	Braised Lamb shanks

Conclusion

The ketogenic diet is a low carb diet designed to put the human body in a high ketogenic state, which could inevitably lead to more intense fat burning and weight loss. This is a fairly affordable diet with various keto foods available in the markets at very low prices. It is not a diet that is more effective for the rich and the elite.

Ketogenic diets offer many vitamins per calorie. However, you still need the same amount of vitamins as your youth. You could have a tougher time living with junk food, not like when you were younger. This approach is essential for consuming foods that guide your health and fight disease. This can help you live an exciting life as you grow up with joy. You want to eat more delicious optimal meals and avoid the moderate, empty calories that appear in high sugar foods like cereals. You want to increase the amount of protein and fat rich in nutrients you eat.

Carb-rich ingredients are pushed using society and aren't beneficial to your long-term health. Carb low diets containing excessive quantities of plant and animal fat are way better for increasing insulin sensitivity. It also slows down cognitive decline, making your overall health higher.

It's no longer too late to enhance your possibilities of functioning and feeling as you get older. You can start doing higher and eating higher. Keto for women over 50 years is another danger to repair some of the damage performed in your younger days while you didn't pay attention to what you did eat.

The in advance you begin to make those changes to enhance your weight, immunity, and blood sugar, the better your chances of living better and longer.

All of us get older. However, we will all control our satisfaction with life as we get even older. Keto diets help you enhance your health so that you can thrive instead of being in pains and illness as you get farther away from fifty.

Again, the keto food plan isn't the handiest diet in global health and wellness. You are afforded a wide variety of alternatives and methodologies that you can choose to undertake for yourself. This type of range and diversity inside the enterprise of weight-reduction plan is continually going to be good. This way, people are going with the intention to discover the weight-reduction plan that first-class fits their very own private wishes and their lifestyles. And if you are one who is contemplating adopting the keto food plan for your personal life, then you're going to need to know just how it compares to different options.

It's proper that there are undoubtedly many weight losses plans obtainable at the market, and it'd be too arrogant to say that the keto weight loss plan is high-quality among them all. The keto eating regimen is a high-quality one for you for my part if it takes place to serve your wishes and your goals higher effectively.

The keto weight-reduction plan also enforces discipline and precision for the agent by incorporating macro counting and meal journaling to ensure accuracy and accountability in the weight-reduction project. There are no external factors that can impact how robust this weight loss plan may be for you. Everything is all within your control.

And finally, it's a reasonably viable weight loss plan, because you don't just compromise on taste or variety. Sure, there are many limitations. But ultimately, there are many alternatives and solutions that can help prevent desire. If these kinds of patterns and reasons apply to you and your personal life, then it would be very safe to say that the keto diet plan is high quality for you.

CPSIA information can be obtained
at www.ICGtesting.com
Printed in the USA
BVHW050102020321
601387BV00013B/1196